101 Must-See Movie Moments

Memorable Scenes in Overlooked Films
and
Overlooked Scenes in Neglected Films

Nell Minow

Miniver Press

Library of Congress Cataloging-in-Publication Data Minow, Nell.

Movie Mom: 101 Must-See Movie Moments

Summary: Nell Minow, the Movie Mom© writes 101 essays about memorable movie moments

ISBN: 978-1-939282-05-7

Published by Miniver Press, LLC, McLean Virginia

Copyright 2012 Nell Minow

Cover design and photo by David Apatoff

Book design and layout by O. Daniel Castillo (sitenb.com)

All rights reserved under International and Pan-American Copyright Conventions. No part of this text may be reproduced, transmitted, down-loaded, decompiled, reverse engineered, or stored in or introduced into any information storage and retrieval system, in any form or by any means, whether electronic or mechanical, now known or hereinafter invented, without the express written permission of Nell Minow. For information regarding permission, write to editor@miniverpress.com

All photos and posters copyright of the individual studios.

First print edition January 2013

To David, who makes every moment memorable.

Contents

	Introduction	i
1.	17 Again (2009)	1
2.	The Adventures of Priscilla, Queen of the Desert (1994)	5
3.	The Adventures of Robin Hood (1938)	7
4.	An Affair to Remember (1957)	11
5.	Ali (2002)	15
6.	Amadeus (1984)	19
7.	American Splendor (2003)	23
8.	Amistad (1997)	27
9.	Annie Hall (1977)	31
10.	Apollo 13 (1995)	35
11.	The Apostle (1997)	39
12.	The April Fools (1969)	43
13.	Awakenings (1990)	47
14.	Bad Day at Black Rock (1955)	51
15.	Ball of Fire (1941)	55
16.	Before Sunrise (1995)	59
17.	Bell Book and Candle (1958)	63
18.	The Best Man (1964)	67
19.	The Best Years of Our Lives (1946)	71
20.	Body and Soul (1947)	75
21.	Boiler Room (2002)	79
22.	Boogie Nights (1997)	81

23.	Boys on the Side (1995)	85
24.	Casa De Los Babys (2003)	89
25.	The Chalk Garden (1964)	93
26.	Charlie Wilson's War (2007)	97
27.	Cold Souls (2009)	101
28.	The Company (2003)	105
29.	The Court Jester (1957)	109
30.	Crash (2005)	113
31.	Die Hard (1988)	117
32.	Diner (1982)	121
33.	Dirty Rotten Scoundrels (1988)	123
34.	Divorce American Style (1967)	127
35.	Dog Day Afternoon (1975)	131
36.	Drumline (2002)	133
37.	Everybody Rides the Carousel (1975)	137
38.	Fade to Black (2004)	139
39.	Father of the Bride (1950)	141
40.	Finding Nemo (2003)	145
41.	The Fisher King (1991)	149
42.	Friendly Persuasion (1956)	153
43.	Galaxy Quest (1999)	157
44.	The General (1926)	161
45.	Giant (1956)	165
46.	The Godfather, Part 2 (1974)	169
47.	Gold Diggers of 1933 (1933)	173
48.	Harper (1966)	175
49.	High Time (1960)	179

50.	Hobson's Choice (1954)	183
51.	Holiday (1938)	187
52.	Homicidal (1961)	189
53.	Hoop Dreams (1994)	193
54.	Houseboat (1958)	197
55.	How Do You Know? (2010)	199
56.	I Love You Again (1940)	201
57.	Inherit the Wind (1960)	205
58.	It's Always Fair Weather (1955)	209
59.	It's a Mad Mad Mad Mad World (1963)	213
60.	The Lady Eve (1941)	217
61.	Lars and the Real Girl (2007)	221
62.	The Last Waltz (1978)	225
63.	A League of Their Own (1992)	229
64.	The Little Colonel (1935)	231
65.	Little Miss Sunshine (2006)	235
66.	Love With the Proper Stranger (1963)	239
67.	The Magnificent Ambersons (1942)	243
68.	Manhunter (1986)	247
69.	The Man Who Shot Liberty Valance (1962)	251
70.	Meet Me in St. Louis (1944)	255
71.	Men in Black (1997)	259
72.	Miss Firecracker (1989)	263
73.	Miss Tatlock's Millions (1948)	267
74.	Moving Midway (2007)	271
75.	Mr. Blandings Builds His Dream House (1948)	275
76.	National Velvet (1944)	279

77.	Notorious (1946)	283
78.	Postcards from the Edge (1990)	287
79.	The Postman Always Rings Twice (1946)	289
80.	Pulp Fiction (1994)	293
81.	Raiders of the Lost Ark (1981)	297
82.	Rich in Love (1992)	299
83.	Rudy|(1993)	301
84.	School Daze (1988)	305
85.	The Shining (1980)	309
86.	Sounder (1972)	313
87.	State Fair (1945)	315
88.	The Story of Us (1999)	319
89.	Stranger Than Fiction (2006)	321
90.	Strangers on a Train (1951)	327
91.	Stuck On You (2003)	331
92.	The Tall Guy (1989)	335
93.	This is Spinal Tap (1984)	337
94.	The Thomas Crown Affair (1968)	341
95.	A Thousand Clowns (1965)	345
96.	Top Gun (1986)	349
97.	Toy Story 3 (2010)	353
98.	Twelve Monkeys (1995)	357
99.	The Wild Parrots of Telegraph Hill (2005)	361
100.	Wives and Lovers (1963)	363
101.	Working Girl (1988)	367
	Acknowledgements	371
	About the Author	375

Introduction

My parents recently came across a letter my dad wrote to my grandfather when I was four, describing my first time in a movie theater. "Nell couldn't have loved it more," he said. "She talks of nothing else and wants to go to the movies all the time."

That never changed. I feel very lucky to have a job where I get to watch movies every day. Each time the lights go down, I still can't wait to see what's on the screen. After watching thousands of films, this book gives me a chance to share some of my all-time favorite movie moments.

I've tried to avoid the scenes everyone already knows in favor of great moments from neglected or flawed movies and overlooked scenes in great movies. Some are moments that demonstrate what movies do best, the purest form of cinematic storytelling. Some are just favorite lines or images, but most are exceptional solutions for challenges all movies must grapple as they try to pack a lot of emotion, action, drama, and characters into a very limited time. Those are challenges like introducing us to the lead characters, making us care about what they are trying to accomplish, or illustrating the passage of time.

Many movies show us characters surprising others (and the audience) with their skill or courage. I will show you why "Amadeus" and "A League of Their Own" do it better than most. What can we learn from the opening credits? If they are designed by Saul Bass, they can be the most creative part of the movie. What do "Notting Hill" and an almost forgotten Bing Crosby movie do to show time passing more effectively than most prestige films? Check out the essay on "High Time." What does DBTA mean and why is Goose from "Top Gun" the best example? Why is it so chilling in

"Strangers on a Train" when everyone in the stands at a tennis game follow the ball except for one?

Two movies made it onto the list because they show us characters reacting to the way something tastes, one played by one of those "face is familiar" character actors and another by one of the most acclaimed movie stars in history.

Powerful scenes in "Annie Hall" "School Daze" and "A League of Their Own" feature characters we see for only a few seconds. We never even learn their names but they are a crucial part of the story. The "B-story" couples are not the center of attention but they get the best moments in "How Do You Know" and "17 Again." What makes a scene work better in some films than others? Many movie heroines transform a tacky dress into high fashion by tearing off some tulle or an overskirt. Who did it best? I think it was Sophia Loren in "Houseboat." Many movies feature montages, compilations of short clips, usually to music, to show us the progress of some project or romance. I've picked two that stand out. And a lot of movies have proposals, apologies, and kisses. I've included some of the best.

There are brilliant musical numbers in the non-musicals "Rich in Love" and "Miss Firecracker." And some of the best moments in "Die Hard" and "Raiders of the Lost Ark" came when directors changed their plans to take advantage of unexpected opportunities or unexpected obstacles while filming with unforgettable results.

You know her as the most acclaimed dramatic actress of her generation, but this book will guide you to Meryl Streep's silliest appearance as a singing Bonnie Parker. You will also have a chance to see some of the biggest Broadway stars of the 1940's show off their best drawing room manner in rare movie appearances.

I love documentaries. There are unforgettable scenes no one expected to capture in "Hoop Dreams" and "The Last Waltz" and one of the sweetest final images ever shown on screen in "The Wild Parrots of Telegraph Hill." In some of the essays I provide background on the film or thoughts on how movies address different challenges. In others, I will just tell you why I think it is worth watching and what to look for.

The single most important attribute for a career in reviewing each week's big studio releases is an infinite capacity for awful movies. We become critics because we love to watch great movies and then we end up sitting through an endless series of buddy cops, gross-out comedies, second-rate superheroes, and remakes of television shows that some studio executive loved as so much as a kid that he had the lunchbox. All those chases and explosions and "run with a gun" stories start to blend together. And yet, almost always I can find some performance, line of dialog, detail of production design, or insight that makes me glad I saw it. Some of those moments are here as well.

For me, movies combine the best of every other art form. They contain elements of writing, theater, music, dance, and graphic design. They can be formal and stylized or intimate and improvised. Movies bring us inside their stories as no other art form can, allowing us to experience what is happening to the characters through the grandest sweep of adventure with marching armies or inter-galactic journeys to the smallest and most private moments with a close-up of a face showing devastating loss or by letting us listen in on whispered words of love and hope. Movies are life without the boring parts. They illuminate the human story by giving us a chance to see one or more characters resolve something that unsettles their lives with a conclusion that can be happy, sad, funny, or bittersweet but somehow gives us a satisfying sense of alignment and understanding.

We see the same stories over and over. A young person leaves home. A stranger comes to town. Two or more people who don't know each other or don't like each other have to accomplish some task, often involving a journey. We hear the same lines over and over. Two that seem to occur in nearly every movie are "Please, try to understand" or "Why don't you try to get some rest." What makes a movie memorable is in the details of plot, direction, cinematography, dialog, performance, lighting, and design that still manage to make these stories distinctive, touching, and authentic. This book includes some of my favorite examples and my thoughts on what makes them stand out.

One of the best things about movies is that while we change, they stay the same. We can come back to them over and over, bringing to them our enlarging understanding and our memories of what they have meant to us over many years.

In this era of almost unlimited access to the entire history of movies, it is easy to track down almost any film, even if it is just to watch one scene. If you have not seen these movie moments, take a look. If you have seen them, watch them again. And write to me at moviemom@moviemom.com to let me know what you think and to share some of your own favorite must-see movie moments. I'd love to hear from you.

101 Must-See Movie Moments

Memorable Scenes in Overlooked Films
and
Overlooked Scenes in Neglected Films

1

17 Again
(2009)

The B-Story Romance

The movie: Films about romance, whether dramas or comedies, often have an "A story" about the hero and heroine meeting, falling in love, facing some conflict, and overcoming it. And then there is the "B story," a counterpoint subplot involving, for example, the best friends of the hero and heroine. If the A story is more serious, the B story will be more comic and vice versa. In "Neptune's Daughter," the movie that introduced the Oscar-winning song, "Baby It's Cold Outside," Ricardo Montalban urges Esther Williams not to leave in a romantic duet while the B couple sings a comic version with Red Skelton trying to leave and Betty Garrett the one who wants him to stay.

Fred Astaire and Ginger Rogers are the A story in "Follow the Fleet," the fifth of their nine co-starring roles. But there isn't much story. This time, they played long-time dance partners (and sometime romantic partners) who are reunited at the beginning of the film. Their dance numbers show their estrangement dissolving as their movement demonstrates their essential rightness for each other. As usual in their films, their non-dancing screen time is low key, partly because after their first film (where they were more like the C story), it was inevitable that they would get together, and partly because Astaire was not interested in trying to be much of an actor. The slightly more dramatic B story involves Roger's character's sister (played by Harriet Hilliard before she married Ozzie Nelson and became the mother of Dave and Ricky) and frequent B-story hunk Randolph Scott.

"17 Again" is a body-switching movie, better than most because of an appealing performance by Zac Efron as Mike O'Donnell, a disappointed middle-aged man who magically turns back into his teenage self, and because of a script with a little more heart and a few more surprises than most of this genre. One of those surprises is the comic but very sweet B story romance between Mike's best friend Ned (Thomas Lennon) and the high school principal, Jane Masterson (Melora Hardin).

When we first meet Mike, in a flashback to his senior year as basketball star and all-around high school success story, we see that in addition to being an athlete with a beautiful girlfriend he is a kind-hearted and brave teenager who sticks up for his dorky friend, Ned. In the present day, Ned is still dorky, but he is also a very wealthy software designer. When Mike is suddenly 17 again, he persuades Ned to pretend to be his father so he can enroll in high school and get a second chance to try to have a better outcome. Ned brings Mike to register for school and is instantly smitten with Jane but she remains completely professional and tells him she does not date her students' parents.

Later their relationship takes a surprising turn when Jane reveals that they have something in common.

The moment: The B story has more heft here (for a light comedy) than most, partly due to the writing and partly due to expert work from two under-appreciated performers. Thomas Lennon is better known as a writer (with Robert Ben Garant, the "Night at the Museum" films and "Reno 911") and is often seen in over-the-top silly roles. Here he makes Ned a real character, not just a silly joke. We can understand why he has been Mike's lifelong friend. Ned may not have a strong grasp of conventional social skills, but he is very loyal and a curious, creative thinker. And Jane is more than the straight-laced principal. Hardin is one of the best comic actresses around. Fans of "The Office" know her as Jan, Michael's supervisor and sometime romantic interest. Here she is a pleasure to watch as a disciplined professional who cannot help but be amused and intrigued by Ned. I love the look on her face as she reveals her own inner fangirl.

Ned Gold: I can't act normal.

Principal Jane Masterson: Clearly.

Ned Gold: I'm just trying to impress you. I don't come to places like this. I'm a dork. I'm the kind of person who spends $10,000 on Gandalf the Grey's quarterstaff from the "Two Towers."

Principal Jane Masterson: Yes that does make you a dork. Especially since Gandalf the Grey only appears in "Fellowship." He returns in "Two Towers" as Gandalf the White.

Made for each other. She even speaks Elvish.

More body-switching:

"Big"

"Freaky Friday" (all three versions)

"Turnabout"

§ § §

2

THE ADVENTURES OF PRISCILLA, QUEEN OF THE DESERT (1994)

I Will Survive

The movie: A low-budget Australian film about two drag queens and a transsexual driving across the country in a broken-down bus called Priscilla became an Oscar-winner, an international box-office sensation, and a Broadway musical. The movie was also an introduction to two talented actors who would go on to star in some of the following decade's most high-profile films and a very different look at an established performer we thought we knew.

Drag queens Tick/Mitzi (Hugo Weaving of "The Lord of the Rings" and "The Matrix" series) and Adam/Felicia (Guy Pearce of "L.A. Confidential" and "Memento") and recently bereaved transsexual Bernadette (Terrence Stamp of "Wall Street" and "Superman II") are on their way to perform at a nightclub in the Australian outback. Like all road trip sagas, that means unexpected encounters and even more unexpected revelations.

But what is really unexpected here is the wildly imaginative vitality of the costumes, which deservedly won an Oscar for Lizzy Gardiner and Tim Chappel and top honors in the British and Australian awards as well. They probably had the smallest costume budget ever to win the Oscar but more than made up for it with outrageous creative flair. Where else will you see a dress made entirely out of flip-flop shoes? Who else could make a flip-flop shoe dress look like it belongs on a couture runway? I love the way the costumes for the final musical numbers take over-the-top to a whole new level, making the characters into exotic lizards that embrace their Australian heritage and showing they are inspired by more than far-away showgirl glitz and Abba songs.

The moment: At one point as they are driving through the desert, they meet a group of Aborigines and decide to put on a show for them. Unlike the homophobic townies they meet at another stop, the indigenous people are welcoming and appreciative. Mitzi, Felicia, and Bernadette dress up and dance to the disco anthem, "I Will Survive" as the Aborigines sit by the campfire.

It is a great number, like all of the musical performances in the film. But what makes this one especially touching is the way the Aborigines wordlessly join in. One accompanies the recorded music on the didgeridoo (performed by Charlie McMahon), adding a haunting breathiness to the hard-edged disco classic.

And even in the dim firelight, the trio recognizes the glint in the eye of an audience member who feels the same longing for glitter and wigs that they do. They dress him up and invite him into the act. Their appreciation of each other and joy in performing is one way this film welcomes us into the world of its characters.

More fabulous movie drag queens:

Wesley Snipes, Patrick Swayze, and John Leguizamo in "To Wong Foo Thanks for Everything, Julie Newmar"

Philip Seymour Hoffman in "Flawless"

Nathan Lane in "The Birdcage"

§ § §

3

THE ADVENTURES OF ROBIN HOOD (1938)

Robin is Bested

The movie: Errol Flynn is the definitive Robin Hood in this gloriously Technicolor version of the classic story, one of the most thrillingly entertaining films of all time and perfect in every detail.

King Richard the Lion-Hearted, off fighting in the Crusades, has been captured and held for ransom. His unscrupulous brother John schemes to make sure Richard never returns, so he can take over as king. All of the knights offer their support to the usurper but one, the gallant Sir Robin of Locksley (Errol Flynn at his most dashing), who vows to raise the ransom money himself and becomes a hunted man.

Robin and his followers use Sherwood Forest as cover so they can steal from the rich and powerful to help the poor and raise the ransom money. They capture a group of travelers that includes the Sheriff of Nottingham (Melville Cooper), Sir Guy of Gisbourne (Basil Rathbone), and the lovely Maid Marian (Olivia de Haviland), the King's ward. Marian is at first scornful, but when she learns that Robin and his men are loyal to Richard, and sees how the Normans have abused the Saxons, she becomes sympathetic.

In order to capture Robin, the Sheriff plans an archery contest, with the prize to be awarded by Marian. They know Robin will not be able to resist. He enters in disguise, but his superb skill reveals his identity, and he is caught and put in the dungeon. With the help of his men and Marian, however, he is rescued in time to help save Richard from John's plot to have him assassinated.

In this story, Robin shows his integrity not just with his allegiance to the king but by his sense of fairness and generosity. Though he is a Norman, he is willing to lose everything he has to protect the poor Saxons. His loyalty is not limited to his own people; rather, he sees everyone who behaves justly as his people. "It's injustice I hate, not the Normans," he tells Marian.

Robin is not only the world's greatest archer and a master swordsman. He has an interesting and multi-layered character, revealed in his interactions with Marian and with his men. He has a strong and clear sense of justice and honor.

He is always respectful of those who deserve it, including the peasants. He is confident and direct, but also unpretentious and even irreverent. When he tells Marian that her manners are not as pretty as her looks, Prince John laughs that this is quite a contrast to Sir Guy, whose feelings for Marian leave him tongue-tied.

The moment: In the scene where Robin first sees Little John, who will become one of his closest allies, Robin fights him for the right to cross the river first, just for the fun of it. And when Little John wins, tossing him into the water, Robin is delighted. "I love a man that can best me!" Here is where we really see Robin's true spirit. He is not threatened by someone who is stronger or faster or smarter than he is, noble or peasant, a sharp contrast to the small spirits of his opponents. Later, he surprises Marian when he asks the Merry Men to decide whether they will keep the money they have stolen or use it to ransom Richard. He knows they will support the king. And he knows by allowing them to decide he will continue to earn their loyalty.

Robin is not especially concerned with goodness or piety; he even steals food from Friar Tuck. But with the poor and weak, he is gentle and considerate and he is, above all, loyal. At the end, when the king asks him what he wants as a reward, all he asks for is amnesty for his men and Marian's hand in marriage.

More classic swashbucklers:

"The Crimson Pirate"

"The Mark of Zorro" (original, Disney series, and remake)

"The Sea Hawk"

§ § §

4

An Affair to Remember (1957)

Arriving in New York

The movie: I suspect that "An Affair to Remember" is more loved than watched. The first third is superb as international ladies' man Nickie Ferrante (Cary Grant) and kept woman Terry McKay (Deborah Kerr) meet on board a luxury cruise ship going to New York, where the people each is supposed to marry are waiting for them.

This was the era of elegant ocean liners with luxurious staterooms, where passengers dined in formal wear. And it was in the time when traveling on these ships meant being completely cut off from the rest of the world, other than the rare ship-to-shore cable. This means that Terry and Nickie have time for some sparkling verbal sparring in some very glamorous settings. Some of those lines were improvised by Irene Dunne and Charles Boyer in the first version of this story, called "Love Affair," made by the same director and co-writer, Leo McCarey in 1939, and some were improvised by Kerr and Grant during filming. The visit to Nickie's grandmother (Cathleen Nesbitt) is charming and filled with quiet grace as we see Terry and Nickie bound together by their appreciation for her simple integrity and wisdom.

They realize they have changed and can no longer marry the wealthy people they are engaged to. But after they get back home and work hard while staying apart for six months and especially after Terry is hit by a car on the way to meet him on top of the Empire State Building, the movie really bogs down for about 45 minutes. You are better off skipping the middle section, especially the part with the singing kids. (Trivia note: Kerr's singing voice is provided by Marni Nixon, who sang for her again in "The King and I" and for Audrey Hepburn in "My Fair Lady" and Natalie Wood in "West Side Story.") Just fast-forward to enjoy that unforgettable last scene when Nickie discovers what really happened to prevent Terry from meeting him, the fabulous, "If it had to happen to one of us, why did it have to be you" moment with the shawl and the painting at the end. That scene is what inspired the loving tribute in "Sleepless in Seattle" and mentions in other films and television shows.

But don't miss the special moment when they arrive at the dock in New York.

The moment: Just before they arrive in New York, Terry and Nickie meet after both have been up all night trying to decide whether they can give up the easy lives they had planned, and figuring out how to make it work. They agree to take six months to prove themselves worthy of one another and then they will meet on top of the Empire State

Building, "the closest thing to heaven there is in New York."

Then they part to get ready to arrive at the dock and there is a perfectly orchestrated little moment when the ship lands in New York. It is wordless, everything in the faces of Grant and Kerr and the camera work and editing directed by McCarey. We go back and forth between Nickie and Terry. They each find and smile and wave at the excited fiancés. They check out each other's intended. They look back and forth at each other to convey curiosity, grudging approval, and longing. And then the camera pulls back and we see that while they have been acting as they though they were alone and unnoticed, everyone on the ship has been watching the whole time, their heads swinging back and forth as though they were watching a tennis match.

Note: The original version is very worthwhile, but the second remake with Warren Beatty and Annette Bening, in 1994, is not, even with Katharine Hepburn as the playboy's grandmother.

More movies on ocean liners:

"Romance on the High Seas"

"Titanic"

"A Night at the Opera"

§ § §

5

ALI
(2002)

A Moment Between Boxers

The movie: Will Smith delivers a knock-out punch as Muhammed Ali in this outstanding film that follows the champ from his first heavyweight title to the "Rumble in the Jungle" when he won the title again by defeating George Foreman in Zaire.

Smith is a great choice to play Ali. Both have pretty faces and easy charm that mask the ferocity and fury that it takes to make it all the way to the top. Ali never trained harder for a fight than Smith did for this role, spending two years packing on muscle and throwing -- and receiving -- real punches in the ring.

Smith also perfectly captures Ali's Kentucky drawl. Like his fighting style, it can float like a butterfly and sting like a bee. Director Michael Mann strikes just the right balance between the personal and the political, setting Ali's struggles in the context of the racial conflicts of his era but never losing sight of the fact that it is one man's story.

Ali repeatedly tells those around him that he will be the champ his own way, and we see him try to figure out what that way will be. He won't be the white man's idea of a "good Negro," like Joe Louis. He will become a Muslim, let Elijah Muhammed's son be his manager and even shun his friend Malcolm X when told to. But he knows that everyone needs him more than he needs them. He will be a Muslim his way, too. He will be more faithful to his refusal to fight than he will be to any of the women in his life. And he will use the force of his personality, more powerful than any punch, to go the distance and get the title. No one can stop him.

Even limited to only 10 years in Ali's life, the story spills out of the screen, with achingly brief glimpses of some of the key characters in Ali's life. This is a double loss, because these small roles are played by some of the most brilliant and under-used actors working today, including Jeffrey Wright as Ali's photographer, LeVar Burton glimpsed briefly as Martin Luther King, Joe Morton as Ali's lawyer, and Giancarlo Esposito as Ali's father. John Voight struggles under far too much rubber make-up but makes a fine impression as Howard Cosell, the sportscaster who was Ali's favorite straight man and one of his truest friends. Mario van Peebles is quietly magnetic as Malcolm X, and Ron Silver marshals his intensity just right as trainer Angelo Dundee. Mykelti Williamson is jubilantly entertaining as Don King.

The moment: Mann is a master of moments that are brilliantly revealing about the characters and themes. Here he shows us how, before a fight, Dundee quietly loads his pockets with first aid equipment, knowing that the brilliantly healthy and fit fighter will soon be needing it between rounds. And in a heartbreaking scene, Ali hugs the just-defeated Jerry Quarry. A moment before they were trying to beat each other senseless. But Ali knows that the bond between them as fighters is what matters. That moment is even more devastating for those aware of Quarry's ultimate fate. He became severely impaired from injuries sustained in boxing matches and died at age 53. It is impossible to watch the movie without thinking of Ali's own injuries and feeling the loss of the resplendently vigorous champ he once was.

More movie boxers:

"Body and Soul"

"Raging Bull"

"Rocky"

§ § §

6

Amadeus
(1984)

Unsuspected Depth

The movie: In my very favorite movie, "The Philadelphia Story," there is a scene where a tipsy reporter named Macaulay Connor (James Stewart in his only Oscar-winning role) pays a late night visit to the wealthy C.K. Dexter Haven (Cary Grant). Connor is brash and suspicious of the upper classes, but when he sees the novel he wrote on Haven's shelf, Connor says appreciatively, "C. K. Dexter Haven, you have unsuspected depth!"

I always think of that line in the scene that seems to come in most movies when one character discovers that another is capable of more than he or she imagined. This includes the moment when Ginger Rogers and Fred Astaire discover mid-dance that they can both dance better than anyone else and are meant to be together on the dance floor and in life forever (see "Swing Time" and "Top Hat"). It includes the scene where Eddie Murphy shows Nick Nolte how he can get what he wants from the racist bartender in "48 Hours."

In two different movies, in equally delightful scenes, beautiful women astonish the men they are dating by demonstrating their musical gifts, one on the trumpet (Kay Kendall in "Genevieve") and one on the drums (Stella Stevens in "The Courtship of Eddie's Father"). In "It Happened One Night," the first film to win all five top Oscars, Claudette Colbert surprises Clark Gable twice, first by her "special" system for getting a car to stop and pick them up by showing her lovely leg, and second by pretending to be a bickering wife to throw the people who are looking for her off the track.

Those scenes remind me of superheroes with secret identities. I think one reason the notion of "unsuspected depth" is so compelling is that we all feel at times as though we have more than people give us credit for. We all feel that others see our Clark Kent personas, never realizing that somewhere there is a Superman inside. Or we would like it to be that way.

What makes the "unsuspected depth" scene in "Amadeus" so resonant is that there is more to it than the usual, "I didn't know he could do that!" For one thing, we already know he could do that. He is Mozart, possibly the most prodigiously talented musician in history. Even though we meet him in this film as a graceless, profane, and immature young man with a braying donkey laugh, we know already that this character has been composing masterpieces since he was a young child and has created some of the most purely glorious music the world will ever know.

So playwright Peter Shaffer wisely made another character the center of the story. We do not see the story through the eyes of Wolfgang Amadeus Mozart, played by Tom Hulce (Amadeus means "loved by God"), the man who is a musical genius but struggles to get the approval of his father and to support his family. It is the story of the man who thought he had achieved everything his ambitious heart has always wanted, Antonio Salieri, played by Oscar-winner F. Murray Abraham.

Salieri is very proud of his prestigious position as Court Composer for Emperor Joseph II (played by Jeffrey Jones, better known as the principal in "Ferris Bueller's Day Off"). Salieri is honored by everyone and surrounded by luxury.

And yet, his curse is that while he does not have enough talent to be truly great, he has enough to understand what no one else does -- that the obnoxious but guileless young man is one of the greatest geniuses of all time. Salieri's agonizing envy is something we can all understand. Ironically, this highly fictionalized story of his despair gave Salieri the one thing he wanted, enduring fame. As a result of this play, his works have begun to be played again for the first time in more than a century.

There is another fascinating layer to the story. Shaffer had an identical twin. Both brothers were playwrights. In their early years, it was Anthony Shaffer who achieved success with the clever "Sleuth" and the screenplay for Alfred Hitchcock's "Frenzy," while Peter Shaffer wrote more complex and ambitious but less successful plays like "The Royal Hunt of the Sun" and "The Private Ear and the Public Eye." It may be that his thoughts about ambition and success and art during this period helped to inspire the themes of this story.

The moment: Salieri has composed a musical welcome for Mozart's arrival at the court, and plays it for the Emperor and his courtiers. Mozart responds warmly, and, having heard it just once, sits down to play it, far more fluidly than Salieri did with his own composition, and without looking at the sheet music.

And then, one musician to another, caught up in the pure pleasure of playing with notes, Mozart begins to improve the piece, turning it from a simple, predictable, forgettable tune to a piece of complexity and brilliance. Of course he has no sense that he has upstaged or embarrassed Salieri. And it is at that moment Salieri is split in half. The true musician in him is thrilled by Mozart. But he is eaten alive by envy that "a boastful, lustful, smutty, infantile boy" should have the genius he so desperately desires.

More unsuspected depth moments:

"Midnight Run"

"The Other Guys"

"It Happened One Night"

7

AMERICAN SPLENDOR
(2003)

Harvey Pekar Looks at His Life

The movie: Harvey Pekar says, "Ordinary life is pretty complex stuff."

His own life was a good example. He had the most ordinary of professions -- he was a file clerk in a veteran's hospital. He lived in the most ordinary of apartments -- dank, drab and cluttered. He had the most ordinary of frustrations -- a woman in front of him at the grocery store's checkout counter takes too long, a look in the mirror provides "a reliable disappointment."

Pekar faced the most minor and the most severe obstacles and problems with the same grumpy pessimism. Yet Pekar, file clerk, freelance jazz critic, comic book author, sometime David Letterman guest, and the subject of a biographical movie, had an extraordinary ability to recognize and communicate the complexity of ordinary life. Like many artists, Pekar might have been too overwhelmed by life to deal with it, but not too overwhelmed to document it.

This unusual biographical film from writer-directors Shari Springer Berman and Robert Pulcini has Paul Giamatti as Pekar but the real Pekar and his wife and friends also appear and comment on what is going on.

Form serves content because Pekar does not hide a single blemish. On the contrary, he seems to wear his flaws somewhere between chip on his shoulder and a badge of honor. His combination of self-awareness and self-obsession can be unsettling. And yet, Pekar's unpretentious candor makes him seem real, honest, even engaging. He may not like being a file clerk, but he is not slumming and he does not feel superior to anyone there, no matter how aware he is of any of their deficiencies. Being a file clerk fills some need in him, perhaps for order and predictability and authenticity. He, himself, does not fit into any category, and the prismatic portrayal is a recognition that we are always messier than the stories about us.

When we first meet Pekar, he is a child out trick-or-treating on Halloween. The other kids are dressed as superheroes, but he is all he will ever be, himself. When that is insufficiently impressive to elicit candy, he gives up. He would rather be the real Harvey Pekar than a pretend comic book hero. What is ironic, of course, is that Pekar became a real comic book hero.

The artists illustrating Pekar's stories are so many and so varied that their differing renditions of Harvey provide one of the movie's themes. Fan and future wife Joyce Brabner arrives at a bus station to meet Pekar for the first time.

She looks around and before she sees the real Pekar (rather, Paul Giamatti portraying him), she sees the ways he was drawn by different artists, trying to put together the Pekar of the comics with the Pekar who wrote them. This prismatic approach to Pekar is ideal for conveying his complex ordinariness.

The moment: In one compelling scene, Pekar the real person is watching Giamatti, the actor portraying him, who is watching actor Donal Logue playing Pekar in a play. Or maybe Logue is playing Dan Castellaneta, the actor who actually played the part of Pekar in that production.

The real-life characters appear as a sort of Greek chorus to comment on the story and on the movie itself. The real Pekar is, of course, reliably disappointed.

More movies about writers:

"The Whole Wide World" (Robert E. Howard)

"Shadowlands" (C.S. Lewis)

"Capote" (Truman Capote)

§ § §

8

AMISTAD
(1997)

Telling A Story

The movie: In 1839, a group of Africans sold into slavery were being transported to the United States on a Spanish ship. Off the coast of Cuba they escaped from their shackles and attacked the crew, leaving two alive to take them back to Africa. The Spanish sailors tricked the Africans and sailed up the coast of the United States until an American naval ship off the coast of Connecticut captures them. The Africans were brought into court to determine their fate. They were claimed as property ("like livestock") by both the Spanish crew and by the American captors.

Roger Baldwin (Matthew McConaughey), a property lawyer persuades abolitionists Theodore Joadson (Morgan Freeman) and Lewis Tappan (Stellan Skarsgaard) that he has a theory that will help the Africans. He argues that it is not a property case at all. The law provides that only the child of slaves can be a slave.

Since the Africans were not born slaves they are free, and their actions were merely self-defense in aid of restoring their freedom. If Baldwin can prove that they were born as free people in Africa, and not, as their captors alleged, slaves in the West Indies, they would not be considered property; they would be considered free human beings.

The trial attracts the attention of President Martin Van Buren (Nigel Hawthorne), who is in the midst of a campaign for re-election and very aware that he will need the support of Southern voters to win. He is under additional pressure from the eleven-year-old queen of Spain, Isabella II, and her ambassador, who raise claims on behalf of the Spanish fleet. When the judge and jury appear sympathetic to the Africans, Van Buren arranges for a new judge to hear the case without a jury.

Meanwhile, the Africans try to understand what is going on around them. Baldwin and Joadson are able to find a man who speaks Mende, the language of Cinqué (Djimon Hounsou) and some of the other Africans so they can communicate.

The lawyers arguing for the Africans win in court and the government appeals. Former President John Quincy Adams (Anthony Hopkins) represents them before the U.S. Supreme Court, where seven of the nine Justices are slaveholders. In a moving and eloquent argument, he persuades the Justices (with one dissenter) that the Africans were free, and that if they had been white, they would have been called heroes for rebelling against those who tried to take that freedom away.

The moment: Adams explains that in court the one with the best story wins. Indeed, we hear many different stories in the course of the movie as each character tries to explain why his view is the right one. In the first courtroom scene we hear several different "stories" about what should happen to the Africans. All of those stories assume that the Africans are property; the only question is whose property they are. Interestingly, as "property," they cannot be charged with murder or theft. One cannot be both property and capable of forming criminal intent. The only issue before the court is where the Africans will go.

As Baldwin begins to tell Joadson and Tappan his "story" of the case, we see them slowly becoming aware of what had always been obvious to us. The Africans cannot be property. They were free, in which case their actions were not only honorable but heroic, in the same category as the rebellion of America's founding fathers, our own "story" about who we are as Americans. Despite the attempts of Van Buren to subvert the legal system established just decades before, the essential commitment to freedom is so much a part of the story that, at least in this one brief moment, justice triumphed.

Adams, whose father was the second President and one of foremost of the Founding Fathers, made that his story. By persuading the Court, he made it ours as well, as director Steven Spielberg does with this movie.

More movies about Supreme Court cases:

"Gideon's Trumpet"

"Separate But Equal"

"The People vs. Larry Flynt"

§ § §

9

Annie Hall
(1977)

Lobsters

The movie: Woody Allen's most acclaimed film won four Oscars: Best Actress, Best Screenplay, Best Director, and Best Picture. It is also one of the best-loved and best-remembered films of all time.

"Annie Hall" is a bittersweet, semi-autobiographical story of the romance between a comic (co-screenwriter/director Allen) and a would-be singer (Allen's former significant other, Diane Keaton, in the title role). Keaton's real name is Diane Hall.

Because it is so autobiographical for both Allen and Keaton, we tend to overlook the crucial contributions of the other people who worked on the film. Co-scriptwriter Marshall Brickman also worked with Allen on some of his greatest films, including "Sleeper" and "Manhattan," as well as his own underrated "The Manhattan Project" and as co-writer of the Tony Award-winning "Jersey Boys." While it is widely reported that Keaton wore her own clothes to create Annie's idiosyncratic-but- stylish look, it was costume designer Ruth Morley who assembled the layered vintage menswear look that made Annie an instant icon.

As important to the film as Allen himself was editor Ralph Rosenblum, who discusses the way the movie came together in his superb book with Robert Karen, *When The Shooting Stops, The Cutting Begins: A Film Editor's Story*. The original cut of the film ran 140 minutes. The version that was released was just 93 minutes, the second shortest Best Picture winner of all time (after the 91-minute "Marty"). Rosenblum writes about Brickman's reaction to the 140-minute version: "I felt that the film was running off in nine different directions. It was a very commentative film -- and Woody of course is brilliant at that -- and it was funny, but, I felt, nondramatic and ultimately uninteresting, a kind of cerebral exercise."

Allen's original idea was to call the film "Anhedonia," a clinical term for the inability to feel pleasure. The decision to switch from a title that referred to Alvy's dismal neurosis to a title that focused on Keaton's character and to make their relationship from beginning to end the central theme of the movie evolved during the editing process.

Jettisoning 50 minutes of material, including a fantasy segment at Madison Square Garden featuring the New York Knicks competing against a team of five great philosophers, and deleting more scenes with other characters gave the story a powerful simplicity of focus. Another contribution by Rosenblum was the structure that moves the story back and forth in time, which gave it a complexity that mirrored the way we store our memories and process our losses.

The moment: Any moment in this magnificent film merits being singled out for special attention. Perhaps the best remembered are Annie's "La-di-da" lines or Christopher Walken as her brother talking about his suicidal impulse or Allen's character Alvy sneezing into a mound of cocaine or his fantasy of appearing to Annie's family as a Hassidic Jew, or Shelly Duvall's character's description of a concert as "transplendent." And then there is the spider in the bathtub scene and Keaton's piercingly sweet performance of "Seems Like Old Times" and Marshall McLuhan's appearance to crush the fatuous pontification of the arrogant professor or the two relationship-defining jokes Allen tells.

But the scene I want to focus on lasts just 30 seconds and

features a character we never really meet. Earlier in the film we see Alvy and Annie trying to cook a lobster and laughing happily as they are both too squeamish and too tender-hearted to put them into the pot. "Talk to them; you speak shellfish," he tells her. She takes pictures of him that we later see on the wall of her apartment, a memory of time together that was intimate and joyful. Later, after they break up, we see him back in the same kitchen, with lobsters, and a new date. He tries to re-create the happiness of the moment he had there with Annie, but this girl is different. She says coolly, "You're a grown man; you know how to pick up a lobster." And she doesn't get his joke.

There has never been a more purely cinematic or heartbreakingly compelling portrayal of the hopelessness and isolation of a lost love.

More from Woody Allen:

"Sleeper"

"Crimes and Misdemeanors"

"Stardust Memories"

"Take the Money and Run"

"Midnight in Paris"

§ § §

10

Apollo 13
(1995)

Working the Problem

The movie: There are two memorable real-life quotations that define this story of a catastrophic accident in space. Jim Lovell, Captain of the Apollo 13 mission, realizes that an explosion has caused severe, possibly fatal damage to the space capsule that is on its way to the moon. He keeps his composure and starts communicating with Mission Control, giving them the information they need to help him and his crew. "Houston, we have a problem," he begins. As things continue to go wrong up in space, head of Mission Control Gene Krantz tells the staff they have to figure out a way to get the astronauts home safely: "Failure is not an option."

Two-time Oscar winner Tom Hanks plays real-life astronaut Jim Lovell on the mission to the moon that almost left three astronauts stranded in space when an oxygen tank exploded. Even though we know it turned out all right, even though the technical material is dense and the action is confined to a space smaller than an elevator, the tension is breathtaking, as the astronauts and the mission control team in Houston try to think their way back home. It is thrilling real-life story of heroism with masterful performances, an outstanding script, and impeccable technical authenticity. More than that, it is a heartening story of the triumph of smart guys who solve problems with intelligence, dedication, and expertise.

Gary Sinise plays Ken Mattingly, who was part of the

crew for the Apollo 13 mission but was replaced at the last minute because he had been exposed to the measles. On the ground, he shows his professionalism and grace by taking over the task of establishing a new procedure that will preserve enough energy to get them home. One important decision is to re-create the conditions inside the spaceship to evaluate the options. Mattingly will not even use a flashlight that is different from the ones his colleagues have in space.

Times have changed. Everyone in Mission Control is a white male (and they all smoke all the time). They are amazed that a computer is small enough to fit into one room. And you may have to the scene where the engineers take out their slide rules -- for kids today, they are more exotic than an abacus.

Lovell's wife is played by Kathleen Quinlan, who was nominated for an Oscar for her performance. She has to tell her mother-in-law in a nursing home that there is a problem with the space capsule and her son is in danger. At first, Blanche (Jean Speegle Howard, real-life mother of director Ron Howard) seems frail and forgetful. But then she looks over at her granddaughter with shrewd asperity and tells her not to be scared. "Don't you worry. If they could get a washing machine to fly, my Jimmy could land it."

The moment: There is no better depiction in film of smart people working hard to solve big problems. As three astronauts struggle to breathe in a tiny space capsule 170,000 miles from earth, Mission Control has to address a series of escalating life-threatening problems. The ground crew has to analyze every item on the ship to determine what uses can be made of equipment designed for other purposes. Everything from duct tape to the cover of the flight manual to one of the astronaut's socks is used, when Mission Control asks simply, "What's good on that ship?" and builds from there to create a filter that will prevent a deadly build-up of $CO2$. The one who figures it out gets that highest of NASA compliments: "You are a steely-eyed missile man."

More astronaut movies:

"From the Earth to the Moon"

"In the Shadow of the Moon"

"The Right Stuff"

"The Dish"

§ § §

11

THE APOSTLE
(1997)

The Dare

The movie: Robert Duvall has been an enthralling screen presence since his first appearance. Without a single line of dialogue he communicated layers of fear, pain, and yearning as Boo Radley in "To Kill a Mockingbird." In "The Godfather" I and II he played consigliere Tom Hagen. He won an Oscar for his performance in "Tender Mercies" as a country singer trying to put his life in order after years of alcoholism. He has played historical figures Robert E. Lee ("Gods and Generals"), Dwight D. Eisenhower ("Ike: The War Years"), Josef Stalin ("The Guard"), and Adolf Eichmann ("The Man Who Captured Eichmann"). He has appeared in westerns ("Lonesome Dove," "Open Range"), science fiction ("THX 1138," "A Handmaid's Tale"), and video games ("The Godfather: Mob Wars" and its sequels). And he was the original Dr. Frank Burns in the movie version of "M*A*S*H."

Duvall has a taciturn quality that conveys a thoughtful reserve. Sometimes it also conveys internal struggles, as in the first movie he wrote and directed, "The Apostle." Duvall wrote the script in the 1980's, inspired by the cadence and faith of preachers he saw in small Southern towns. He could not get a movie studio to finance it, so he ended up creating his own production company and spending his own money to get it made.

Hollywood films generally portray clergy one-dimensionally as saints, fools, or sinners. But in "The Apostle," as writer, director, and star, Duvall creates a complicated character who is sincere in his faith but struggles with his flawed nature. He plays Euliss "Sonny" Dewey, who is better in his job as a Southern Pentecostal preacher than he is as a husband. His estranged wife (superbly played by Farrah Fawcett) is having an affair. He becomes enraged and attacks her lover with a baseball bat, and then runs away.

Partly because he is hiding from facing the consequences of what he has done, but more because he truly wants a rebirth, he takes a new name, The Apostle E.F. He finds a new community and starts a new church.

The movie has an intimate, improvisational quality that erases the distance we might feel from these characters. Sonny is a man of great compassion and conviction but he also has great anger and jealousy. He has a messianic zeal that may not always come from a place of humility and grace. But, because of his own struggles he has great compassion and he has an unquestionable ability to inspire others to a deeper connection with God.

The moment: Billy Bob Thornton appears in the film as another man who is wrestling with angels. He is deeply disturbed by Sonny's modest new church because it has both black and white worshippers. He arrives driving a bulldozer to knock it down.

In a scene Thornton told me was completely improvised by him and Duvall, Sonny throws his Bible in front of the bulldozer to stop the character known only in the credits as "troublemaker" from going forward. The troublemaker belligerently says he can move the Bible. Sonny gets the congregation to repeat after him, "Nobody moves that book." Then he bends over next to the troublemaker, and puts his hand on the man's back, and speaks to him quietly. "You didn't come here to knock down the church," he says. "You came for something else. You're a good man." Sonny says he will pray with him, he will cry with him.

The authenticity of his understanding, rooted in Sonny's own flaws, opens the troublemaker's spirit. As someone once said, a heart that has been broken can hold the whole world.

More movie clergy:

"Elmer Gantry"

"Leap of Faith"

"A Man Called Peter"

"The Bishop's Wife" (and the remake, "The Preacher's Wife")

"What If"

§ § §

12

The April Fools
(1969)

Wise Counsel

The movie: "The April Fools" is a 1969 film starring Jack Lemmon and Catherine Deneuve that, if remembered at all, is thought of as a dated mid-century mid-life crisis romance and a clumsy attempt by Hollywood to make something that was, to use a briefly popular term of the era, "relevant."

Lemmon plays Howard Brubaker, a good man who tries to do his best but is not quite sure how he got caught up in the phony notions of success he seems stuck with. No one else is questioning it, so he hardly lets himself be aware of how unsatisfied he is. He is married to a woman who seems to care only about renovating houses (Sally Kellerman of "M*A*S*H"). His boss (Peter Lawford) encourages him to find happiness the way he has, by having a lot of affairs. When Brubaker politely asks a woman at the party (Deneuve as Catherine Gunther) if he can buy her a drink she takes it as an invitation to leave the party and he is nonplussed. And he is even more so when he finds himself falling in love with her. What he does not know is that she is married to his boss.

They spend an evening that will lead them both to realize how much they had been missing and how dishonest they had been with themselves.

Lemmon was so good in outlandish roles like "The Great Race" and "Some Like It Hot" it is easy to forget that no one was better at playing a decent guy struggling with the challenges of modern life and trying to do the right thing. Deneuve is never entirely comfortable with the English dialog, but she is so serenely gorgeous it does not really matter.

The moment: It is a pleasant, if bittersweet little trifle, but one scene makes it worthwhile -- when Howard and Catherine meet an older couple who more by example than by anything they say make them think seriously about where they want to be and who they want to be with. And that couple is magnificently portrayed by two of the all-time greats, Charles Boyer and Myrna Loy.

Joseph Campbell wrote about the prevalence in myth of "the old man in the woods," the character sought out by the hero to help guide him on his journey. Think of Yoda in "The Empire Strikes Back" or Professor Falken in "Wargames" or "Deep Throat" in "All the President's Men" or Dumbledore in the Harry Potter films or Aslan in the Narnia movies or the psychiatrist in "Ordinary People." These are the hero's corner men, the ones who throw water on his face and rub his shoulders and get him back in the ring swinging. "The April Fools" is a particularly good example because as the characters played by Boyer and Loy show the younger couple how much they appreciate what they have together. We also get a sense of the older generation of actors passing the torch to Lemmon and Deneuve.

Brubaker and Catherine go to the club the boss recommended, an outlandish place with a jungle theme, where animal-skin waitresses are summoned by shooting a popgun at their rear ends. They leave for a disco, where they meet Grace (Loy) and when her driver turns out to be drunk, they take her back to her home. There they meet her husband André (Boyer), who explains that nothing good happens during the day (the sun beats down, people have to work), so he has chosen to live at night (women are beautiful, there is champagne to drink).

This is just one of the ways in which Brubaker and Catherine have entered an upside-down world that encourages and enables them to think about what is possible for them. Grace tells Catherine her fortune, smiling that "it's bad luck to be superstitious but the cards are so pretty" and guiding her to have the courage to insist on being happy. But the most important way Grace and André guide Brubaker and Catherine is by showing them that there is such a thing as sustaining, enduring love. Whether it is Grace and André or Loy and Boyer, we cannot help being moved and inspired by the example of these wise and beautiful souls.

More from Myrna Loy:

"The Best Years of Our Lives"

"Libeled Lady"

"I Love You Again"

"Mr. Blandings Builds His Dream House"

More from Charles Boyer:

"Love Affair"

"Gaslight"

"Barefoot in the Park"

§ § §

13

Awakenings
(1990)

The Dance

The movie: There is something especially daunting in studying the brain itself with only our own brains to help us try to comprehend. Oliver Sacks is a neurologist who writes about his patients with the skill of a poet and the heart of one, too. We learn as much from his insight and compassion as from his diagnoses. Often these insights come from observing impairments, some astonishingly particular, that his patients struggle with. And we learn a great deal about the human spirit from the way they respond to these challenges, and the way that Sacks tells their stories.

"Awakenings" is based on a book by Sacks about his work with post-encephalitic patients in the 1960's. They were survivors of a 1920s encephalitis lethargica epidemic that left them "locked-in," very limited in movement and unable to speak. When Sacks began to work with them on a chronic ward in a mental hospital, forty years after their original illnesses, he experimented by giving them the then-new drug that was being used to treat Parkinson's disease. The effect was remarkable. Like a ward full of Sleeping Beauties, they woke from the deep trance they had been in for decades. But the medication's effects were fleeting and before long they were back in an impenetrable trance.

The book inspired a play by Nobel laureate Harold Pinter called "A Kind of Alaska" and a BBC documentary. It also inspired this sensitive, touching, and bittersweet film by screenwriter Steve Zallian ("Schindler's List" and "Searching for Bobby Fischer") and director Penny Marshall ("A League of Their Own").

Robin Williams plays Dr. Sayers (based on Sacks) and Robert de Niro is his patient, Leonard Lowe, who first became ill when he was a bright young schoolboy. His mother still visits him every day after decades of being "locked-in." The hospital administrators think of these patients as incurable, but Sayers sees a connection between their symptoms and Parkinson's. He gets permission from Mrs. Lowe to try L-dopa on Leonard. When it is successful, donors provide money to give the medication to the other patients. Like Leonard, they awaken to find that they have lost forty years.

They are thrilled to be alive but many are horrified to find what they have lost. And then Leonard, the first of their group to "awaken," finds the medication growing less effective. He develops tics. He becomes agitated, emotional, even paranoid. The other patients see in him what lies ahead for them.

Penelope Ann Miller plays Paula, the daughter of a patient in the hospital who is paralyzed and silent following a

stroke. Leonard meets her in the cafeteria when he first becomes "awakened" and she does not realize he is a patient, giving him a poignant glimpse of what it could be like to be "normal." Paula confides in him that she does not know if her father can understand her when she reads the sports pages aloud to him, and Leonard assures her that he does.

The moment: When the medication begins to wear off, Leonard, knowing that he will soon return to his catatonic state, sits with Paula in the cafeteria. She politely pretends not to notice his severe tremors. He puts out his hand to say goodbye for one last handshake. She gets up, places his hand on her waist, takes his other hand, and dances with him, a moment of heart-wrenching poignancy. We feel that both of them share a lifetime in those few seconds.

Pay attention to man playing the piano player, another "locked-in" patient responding to the medication. It is jazz great Dexter Gordon.

More Miller:

"Kindergarten Cop"

"The Freshman"

"Chaplin"

"The Artist"

§ § §

14

BAD DAY AT BLACK ROCK (1955)

What is Big Enough to Make You Mad?

The movie: With themes taken from classic Westerns, film noir, "issue" films and personal redemption, "Bad Day at Black Rock" is a gripping story that resonates on many levels.

It begins, as stories often do, with a stranger coming to town. For the first time in four years, a train stops in a dusty, isolated, desert station called Black Rock. A man wearing a suit gets off the train. His name is John McReedy (Spencer Tracy) and he is the source of great curiosity and surprising hostility, especially when he does not explain what he wants. The hotel tells him all rooms are booked, when that is obviously not true. A hot-headed young tough guy (Lee Marvin) threatens him, then laughs when he sees McReedy has a disabled arm.

McReedy is looking for a resident of the town named Kokomo. This makes the locals even more uneasy. They tell McReedy Mr. Kokomo was sent to the Japanese internment camps at the start of World War II. He knows that is not true. As he insists on finding out what really happened, the secret that has been poisoning the town becomes even more toxic.

The screenplay is based on a short story by Howard Breslin but there is one significant difference, added not to enhance the story but to entice the actor. At the last minute, as Tracy was hesitant to accept the role, producer (and later head of MGM) Dore Schary told the screenwriters to give McReedy a disabled arm because he knew that actors find it very hard to resist the challenge of playing a character with a disability.

Tracy agreed to do the film and the performance is one of his best. The character's disabled arm is a crucial element of the film, dramatically and thematically. It makes McReedy more vulnerable and unsure of his own ability.

Like the people of Black Rock and McReedy himself, we in the audience make the mistake of underestimating him. The internal struggle of the character is made palpable. And it is symbolic of that post-war moment as America dealt with its losses and had to consider thoughtfully its re-dedication to its core principles.

The rest of the cast is outstanding, especially Robert Ryan as Reno Smith, the man who runs things in Black Rock. The screenplay by Millard Kaufman, himself a decorated veteran, is superbly structured and the dialog crackles as the characters circle one another menacingly.

The moment: In a key and very revealing confrontation, Smith tells McReedy that his curiosity is sparked by McReedy's sanguine responses with a line that tells us a lot

about them both: "I believe a man is as big as what'll make him mad. Nobody around here seems big enough to get you mad."

Not a bad way to measure someone.

More from Spencer Tracy:

"Captains Courageous"

"Libeled Lady"

"Guess Who's Coming To Dinner"

§ § §

15

BALL OF FIRE
(1941)

A Professor Proposes to a Showgirl

The movie: I can't figure out why the utterly delightful "Ball of Fire" is not better known. It was directed by Howard Hawks, usually remembered for tough guy movies like "The Big Sleep," "To Have and Have Not," and "Rio Bravo." But he was also the man behind brassy, colorful romps like "Gentleman Prefer Blondes," "Man's Favorite Sport?" and "His Girl Friday" as well as the quintessential screwball comedy, "Bringing Up Baby." And it was written by the incomparable rapier wits behind "Some Like it Hot," the American Film Institute's pick for the number one comedy of all time. "Ball of Fire" is almost as funny, though the comedy is less physical and more verbal, subtler, and without the gender-bending outrageousness. And it has my candidate for the all-time wittiest line of movie dialogue ever. I will reveal that below, but the moment I want to pay tribute to here is a different one.

The story is said to have been inspired by Snow White. It is about a showgirl who hides out with what she calls "seven squirrely cherubs," a group of sheltered single male professors who have been cloistered together in one big house while writing an encyclopedia funded under the terms of a wealthy man's will. They are played by the best of the MGM middle-aged male extras, including S.Z. "Cuddles" Sakall, Oscar Holmoka, Henry Travers (Clarence the angel in "It's a Wonderful Life"), and Richard Haydn.

As the movie begins, the professors are behind schedule, only up to the letter "S." So, the botanist is writing about strawberries. The biologist is writing about sex. And the professor of English and grammar (Gary Cooper as Bertram Potts) is writing about slang. A chance encounter with the local garbage collector convinces him that the academic sources he has been relying on are out of date and so, for the first time in seven years, he must leave to do some field research and listen to the way people really talk.

Potts eavesdrops on students and commuters and then stops in at a nightclub where he sees Sugarpuss O'Shea (Barbara Stanwyck) singing "Drum Boogie." (Watch for Gene Krupa's sensational "Matchstick Boogie" encore.) Mesmerized by her command of the vernacular, he invites her to come in for an interview. She refuses. But then, when the cops want to talk to her about her boyfriend, a gangster known as Joe Lilac (Dana Andrews), she decides the perfect place to hide would be staying with a bunch of encyclopedia-writing scholars. So she talks her way into moving in with the professors for a while.

This is where my favorite line comes in. She is trying to persuade the professors that she can't leave because she has a raspy throat. The professor of medicine peers into her mouth and says with more hope than accuracy that he does see "a slight rosiness." "A slight rosiness?" she repeats. "It's as red as The Daily Worker and just as sore." The cleverness of that pun exemplifies the wordplay throughout the script, a love letter to the English language from Billy Wilder, a screenwriter who did not learn English until he came to the U.S. as an adult.

The moment: That love for language is also reflected in Professor Potts' proposal to Sugarpuss. He gives her a ring and asks her to read the inscription. "Richard ill?" She asks. "Richard III," he gently corrects her.

There was not room for the entire quotation, so he has only had the citation inscribed in the ring. He recites the line from memory.

> *Look, how this ring encompasseth thy finger,*
> *Even so thy breast encloseth my poor heart;*
> *Wear both of them, for both of them are thine.*

It is unlikely a real professor of literature would use that quote because in the play, Richard says those beautiful words for political gain, not romance. But in the context of this film, to use a line from "Drum Boogie," the cat's a killer-diller.

More English professors in movies:

Michael Douglas in "Wonder Boys"

Emma Thompson in "Wit"

Luke Wilson in "Tenure"

Dennis Quaid in "Smart People"

§ § §

16

Before Sunrise (1995)

Magic in the Space in Between

The movie: Oscar-winning screenwriter William Goldman ("All the President's Men," "Butch Cassidy and the Sundance Kid," "The Princess Bride"), commented on a widely circulated anonymous list of movie conventions that we take for granted even though they are completely unrealistic: characters almost always find a parking space, have correct change, and, as soon as they turn on the television or radio immediately hear something directly relevant to whatever situation they are in, and so forth. Goldman explains that this is simply a matter of economy in storytelling. A feature film screenplay is usually about 100 pages long and the average running time is under two hours. There simply is not enough time to show us anything that is not strictly relevant to wherever the narrative is taking us. Movies are life without the boring parts. Everything we see has to move the story forward.

For that reason, there are two widely used conventions for showing us that two characters are in love. After the "meet cute" that captures our interest, either there is a moment where they both discover they have the same favorite poem/hobby/outfielder/flavor of ice cream or some other indicator of their shared view of the world ("17 Again" is a good example) or there is a falling-in-love montage, with a pop song playing as we see them laughing over the selections in an open market, riding bicycles, and frolicking on the beach. Sometimes both.

Again, this is for reasons of economy. We need to establish that they are right for each other so we can get to the story of the movie, which is about whatever is keeping them apart. But it is for another reason, too. Falling in love is very difficult to depict and highly personal. It is extremely hard to show it in a way that will be creative and feel true. This is not a problem that is new to movies. Even Shakespeare wasted no time in having Romeo and Juliet fall in love at first sight. They took one look at each other and immediately started speaking in an extemporaneous joint sonnet, showing us they were meant to be together. That lovely balcony scene that comes later is just clarification and logistics, exquisitely expressed in iambic pentameter.

But "Before Sunrise" is different, which is why it is so cherished. The entire movie is what most films would cover in a three-minute montage. American college student Jesse (Ethan Hawke) and French college student Celine (Julie Delpy) meet on a train and when he impulsively invites her to get off with him in Vienna she impulsively accepts. They walk around Vienna all night long and then they say goodbye and he leaves to return to America.

Co-writer/director Richard Linklater ("Waking Life," "School of Rock," "Dazed and Confused," "Me and Orson Welles") was inspired by an evening he once spent with a girl, walking and talking until the sun came up. The conversation here is wide-ranging and intimate in a way that only happens when there is a strong chance you might never see each other again. They often disagree. But we can see that they have some very important things in common, starting with a very strong, immediate attraction, the willingness to be impulsive, and an openhearted passion for connecting through ideas. Now, that's romantic.

The moment: Celine says: "I believe if there's any kind

of God it wouldn't be in any of us, not you or me but just this little space in between. If there's any kind of magic in this world it must be in the attempt of understanding someone sharing something. I know, it's almost impossible to succeed but who cares really? The answer must be in the attempt." It is a lovely statement and might just as well be coming from Linklater himself about his attempt to connect with us in the audience.

Linklater, Hawke, and Delpy reunited for a 2004 sequel, "Before Sunset," bittersweet but also ravishingly romantic. All three of them collaborated on the script. Intriguingly, they also reunited for a segment in Linklater's trippy animated philosophical exploration, "Waking Life" (2001) that seems to exist in a parallel universe, or perhaps is intended to take place sometime in the future, long after Celine and Jesse's reunion for the first time in nine years in Paris in 2004. The third in the series, "Before Midnight," was released in 2013.

More great films about falling in love:

"And Now My Love"

"Eternal Sunshine of the Spotless Mind"

"Say Anything"

"It Happened One Night"

"Brokeback Mountain"

§ § §

17

BELL BOOK AND CANDLE (1958)

Jimmy Stewart's Eyes

The movie: Every ten years the magazine *Sight and Sound* publishes surveys of critics, ranking the greatest films of all time. In 2012 the long-time Number One, "Citizen Kane," was toppled by Alfred Hitchcock's 1958 film, "Vertigo," a moody love story about loss, vulnerability, identity, and obsession, starring James Stewart and Kim Novak.

The same year, Stewart and Novak also starred in a literally bewitching light romantic comedy that also deals with a kind of obsession. It will never show up in the *Sight and Sound* list, but it is filled with charm and has Stewart's last performance as a romantic lead. He was twice Novak's age and turned 50 while filming, and he decided he was too old to play those roles any more. In both this film and "Vertigo" the age difference bolsters the themes, though, and it is fascinating to see how it can amplify the intensity of the obsession in both a dramatic and comic context.

Novak plays Gillian Holroyd, an art gallery owner. The humans around her do not know she is a witch. Her cat Pyewacket is not a pet but a familiar who strengthens her powers.

When she finds out that her neighbor Shep Henderson (Stewart) is engaged to her college nemesis, Gillian decides to spite her by casting a love spell on Shep. At first, he is happily in love with Gillian, until he finds out how it happened. And Gillian discovers that a witch who falls in love loses her powers and becomes human.

The leads are excellent and there is an exceptionally strong supporting cast, including Jack Lemmon as Gillian's brother, Elsa Lanchester as her aunt, Hermione Gingold as another witch, and television pioneer Ernie Kovacs as a popular author who has written a book about witches.

The moment: Shep finds another witch to give him an antidote to the love spell. Watch Stewart's eyes as he drinks the potion and especially the way his eyes convey horror, resolve, and sheer incredulity. He also makes it very funny.

People who study film often talk about "the gaze" as one of cinema's most compelling techniques. Actors have been performing since people have been telling stories, but it was not until the invention of film that we saw how an intimate close-up of a character can communicate powerfully with just a look and an expression. Watch Stewart's eyes in his scenes with Novak, too. He was almost alone among movie stars in the way he looked into another actor's eyes with absolute steadiness, without any involuntary tracking, the switching from eye to eye that we all do without being aware of it. It is

a simple technique that adds a great deal to the power of his performances.

Most descriptions of Stewart focus on his amiable integrity as an actor, and his accessibility. Because his distinctive mannerisms were consistent from role to role it is easy to categorize him as a movie star who essentially played himself on screen. But comparing the two films he made in the same year with the same co-star is a powerful reminder what a subtle, committed, and superb actor he really was.

More beautiful movie witches:

>Veronica Lake in "I Married a Witch"

>Robin Tunney, Neve Campbell, Fairuza Balk, and Rachel True in "The Craft"

>Billie Burke in "The Wizard of Oz"

>Mila Kunis and Michelle Williams in "The Great and Powerful Oz"

18

THE BEST MAN
(1964)

Shelly Berman's Cross-Examination

The movie: There have been many movies about politics in the United States. What makes "The Best Man" exceptional is that it was written by Gore Vidal, who is both a brilliant writer with a passion for history and a political insider. His grandfather was a Senator. He shared a stepfather with Jacqueline Kennedy Onassis and his cousin Al Gore became a Senator and then Vice President of the United States. He ran for Congress unsuccessfully himself. He wrote novels, essays, and the Tony-award winning play that became the basis for this film about the battle between candidates at a political convention.

Many elements of the story are as true today as when they were written, applicable not just to political power plays but to business, academia, any arena where people battle. But some aspects of the story have more in common with the whistle-stop campaigns and smoke-filled rooms of the 19th century than they do with today's Presidential elections. The play was written at a time before the primary system and the yearlong slog to the nomination, before billion-dollar fundraising and long before the 24-hour news cycle with infinite outlets and voices without any pretense of objectivity or fact-checking.

The two leading candidates for the nomination from the unnamed party are the intellectual and principled William Russell (Henry Fonda), said to be inspired by Adlai Stevenson, and Joe Cantwell (Cliff Robertson), a smooth populist with bombastic anti-Communist views and a ruthless side. He is said to be inspired by John F. Kennedy with a bit of Richard Nixon and Joseph McCarthy added in.

Russell has an estranged wife (back in the days when that was unacceptable in a candidate). He persuades her to pretend to be the supportive wife voters will want to see.

Neither has a majority of the votes going in, so they are competing for endorsements from influential party leaders, especially the ailing former President (inspired by Harry Truman and beautifully played by Lee Tracy).

Each has information on the other that is potentially career-killing. Cantwell's brother has obtained some records of Russell's treatment by a psychologist and is willing to release them, knowing it will make Russell un-electable. And Russell's aides have found someone named Sheldon Bascomb (Shelly Berman) who was in the military with Cantwell and will testify that Cantwell was associating with soldiers who were discharged for being gay. Russell refuses to make use of the smear until he learns how ruthless Cantwell is.

The moment: Shelly Berman was a stand-up comedian who sometimes acted. While he has appeared in other films, his brief appearance in "The Best Man" is his most significant dramatic role on screen, and his performance, even up against Oscar-winning movie stars Fonda and Robertson, is riveting. This small gem of a scene is a movie on its own as Bascomb tells his story, brimming with resentment, excited to be the center of attention but squirming under the scrutiny. When Cantwell takes over the questioning and pins Bascomb like an insect, Berman seems to shrivel before our eyes.

More cross-examination:

"Witness for the Prosecution"

"Anatomy of a Murder"

"My Cousin Vinny"

§ § §

19

THE BEST YEARS OF OUR LIVES (1946)

Retrofitting

The movie: A Best Picture Oscar winner, "The Best Years of Our Lives" captures its moment beautifully but still feels vitally engaging and timely. It is not just the story of three men returning from military service in World War II. It is the story of three characters struggling to adjust to transitions that are far more complex than they had imagined. For so long, they dreamed of coming home. Now they must learn that home is not what they remembered and they are not the same, either. Dreams that come true can still require complicated, even terrifying, adjustments.

This is a beautiful and touching film with a great feeling for its characters. Al (Fredric March) is a middle-aged banker turned infantryman. While he was away, his children grew up. Fred (Dana Andrews) is a soda jerk from a poor family turned decorated bombardier with a pretty wife he barely knows. And Homer (Oscar-winner Harold Russell) is returning home with mechanical hooks to replace the hands he lost in combat.

The movie is filled with wonderfully constructed and performed scenes, including Al's unexpected arrival home, joy followed by awkwardness followed by taking everyone out for drinks. The morning after, when he wakes up with a hangover and his wife Milly (Myrna Loy) brings him breakfast in bed, there is a deeply tender scene when they finally begin to reconnect. Homer is afraid his disability will shock or disgust his longtime sweetheart, the girl next door (Cathy O'Donnell). He finally admits that to himself and gives her a chance to see how his prostheses work in a touching scene where he allows her to button his pajama top.

Fred has the most difficult struggle. He does not fit in at home, with his father and stepmother, or at his old job as a soda jerk. The woman he impetuously married is a frivolous party girl who likes him less now that he is out of uniform and expects her to stay home. The drug store where he worked has been sold to a chain. He suffers from nightmares due to what we now call post-traumatic stress disorder. And he finds himself falling for Al's daughter Peggy (Teresa Wright).

The moment: Everything seems to be falling apart for him and he goes back to the last place he thought would feel like home. At a nearby airport, bomber planes like the one he flew in are lined up, waiting to be junked. He crawls inside one, remembering his time in combat and wondering if he will ever have a sense of mastery and purpose again. Strangely, it feels more like home to him than the town where he grew up.

A man comes over to the plane and yells at him because no one is supposed to be there. The planes are not going to be discarded; they are going to be broken down and turned into materials for housing, an updated version of beating swords into plowshares. Fred realizes that he, too, can be retrofitted for peacetime work. Just as he learned to be a bombardier, he can learn whatever he needs to be a part of the post-war world. He gets a job with the builder who is taking the planes. It is a turning point for Fred with a meaningful metaphor about the opportunities and challenges of the post-war era or indeed any time of turmoil.

More movies about the readjustment of returning military:

"Coming Home"

"The Welcome"

"The Men"

"Til the End of Time"

"The Messenger"

§ § §

20

BODY AND SOUL
(1947)

Canada Lee

The movie: Brian Cady of "Turner Classic Movies" wrote, "Gritty realism, harsh lighting and a cynical view of the sport became the standard for fight films after the popular success of 'Body and Soul.'" The great cinematographer James Wong Howe literally wore roller skates when he took the camera into the boxing ring so that the camera could follow the action.

In a classic parable of corruption and redemption, John Garfield plays Charlie Davis, who becomes a boxer to get money for his mother, but is seduced by the world of money, glamour, and power. After Charlie's father is killed, his mother wants him to get an education. But Charlie is too proud to accept welfare and too angry and impatient to wait. "Tell Quinn to get me a fight. I want money, you understand? Money, money." His mother tries to stop him. "I forbid it. Better you should buy a gun and shoot yourself." "You need money to buy a gun," he responds.

Charlie wins a series of small-time fights and is approached by a gangster who offers him a shot at the big time. His friend warns him to stay away. "He doesn't care about you. He just wants his piece of the pie." "What's the difference?" Charlie replies. "It'll be a bigger pie, more slices for everybody." Charlie drops his girlfriend for a nightclub performer who once dated the mobster and starts enjoying the high life until things start to go badly.

All of the performances are intense and gripping, especially Garfield, who was so passionate about making the movie that he suffered a heart attack and a head injury requiring stitches during filming. Anne Revere as Charlie's mother, Lili Palmer as his girlfriend, and Canada Lee as a former champion, are all superb.

Garfield played an important role behind the scenes as well. He turned down a contract renewal from Warner Brothers to start his own film company, Enterprise Productions, dedicated to making socially relevant and meaningful films. "Body and Soul," inspired by the real-life story of boxer Barney Ross, was its first film.

This is a rare, almost unprecedented film for its era because of its respectful portrayal of an African-American character. Director Robert Rossen, who had boxed a bit himself, met Lee years before and told him he wanted to make a boxing movie. Lee said, "Sign me up." It took a while, but when Rossen had a chance to "Body and Soul" for Enterprise a few years later, he remembered Lee's interest and contacted him. According to his biography, *Becoming Something: The Story of Canada Lee* by Mona Z. Smith, Lee was excited about working on the film because of the progressive political views of everyone associated with it. He felt confident that if any of the action or dialog was demeaning, he would not hesitate to speak up and have it changed. Smith writes that Lee's character, Ben "emerges as the moral conscience of the film, its most sympathetic character, and the white champ's only true friend. These qualifies push Ben's character dangerously close to the cliché of the faithful servant, the Uncle Tom, but Canada found Ben intelligent, courageous, and honest; the actor was convinced that the script showed the black fighter to be Charlie's equal, not his menial."

Garfield's commitment went beyond Lee and his character. He hired a diverse group of actors and crew members, with thirty black actors as extras and bit players. Lee and Garfield became close, with a shared passion for social change. Lee felt that Garfield was especially generous. Smith quotes him: "He constantly wanted to help me. We had some scenes together that he could have turned around for himself -- after all, he's a big star -- but he insisted they were my scenes." When Garfield inadvertently called Lee's character "boy" in one scene, he insisted it be reshot so he could correct the mistake. And Rossen made sure Ben was an essential part of the story even though he knew that would keep the film out of some theaters in the South. In that era, they only showed movies if they could cut out the scenes with black characters.

The moment: This is a rare film made before the 1960s that treats a black character (albeit a tragic one) with dignity and Lee's performance as the doomed former champion has a powerful dignity and grace. Bosley Crowther's original review of the film in the New York Times said,

> It is Canada Lee, however, who brings to focus the horrible pathos of the cruelly exploited prizefighter. As a Negro ex-champ who is meanly shoved aside, until one night he finally goes berserk and dies slugging in a deserted ring, he shows through great dignity and reticence the full measure of his inarticulate scorn for the greed of shrewder men who have enslaved him, sapped his strength and then tossed him out to die. The inclusion of this portrait is one of the finer things about this film.

More from Canada Lee:

Alfred Hitchcock's "Lifeboat"

"Cry, the Beloved Country"

21

Boiler Room
(2002)

Cold Call

The movie: Ben Younger was inspired to write his first screenplay by an interview with a brokerage firm that was clearly a scam. Instead of pursuing the job, he wrote and directed the movie about the high-adrenalin world of "boiler room" securities firms that operate on the edge and over the edge of the law. They "pump and dump" - they sell stock with poor prospects by making unrealistic claims about its prospects as an investment and get rid of their shares before they decline in value.

Seth Davis (Giovanni Ribisi) sets the stage for us at the beginning.

> *The Notorious BIG said it best: "Either you're slingin' crack-rock, or you've got a wicked jump-shot." Nobody wants to work for it anymore. There's no honor in taking that after school job at Mickey Dee's, honor's in the dollar, kid. So I went the white boy way of slinging crack-rock: I became a stockbroker.*

Seth is a college student who makes a lot of money running an illegal gambling operation. So for him, the brokerage job seems like a step forward into a legitimate way of making money. Hurt by the disapproval of his father, a judge, Seth is drawn to the testosterone-fueled brotherhood of the brokers, not realizing that he is closer to slinging crack than he thought. "Originally, I got in for the cash. But getting my dad's respect - that's what kept me there."

There is something heady at first about the take-no-prisoners approach of the brokers, especially when Seth discovers that he has a real gift for selling. But he begins to see that the other brokers are not very happy. They make a lot of money but they do not seem to have much of a life beyond selling. In one scene, a bunch of them visit the big, near-empty house of one of the brokers. He does not have the time or the ability to furnish it. They can all watch "Wall Street" together, reciting all of Gordon Gekko's lines along with the movie. Soon Seth realizes that the operation itself is going down faster and uglier than the crummy penny stocks they are selling.

The moment: Seth is at home eating breakfast when the phone rings. It is a telephone solicitor, trying to sell him a newspaper subscription. He turns him down but then cannot resist passing along some of what he has learned. He gives the guy on the other end of the phone an unforgettable lesson in what it means to be a salesman. And then he turns him down again.

More movies about salesmen:

"Glengarry Glen Ross"

"The Big Kahuna"

"Salesman"

"The Pursuit of Happyness"

§ § §

22

Boogie Nights
(1997)

Pool Party

The movie: "Boogie Nights" is a film of stunning scope and maturity and a masterpiece of pure moviemaking. Writer/director Paul Thomas Anderson sets a quintessential rise and fall story of a young man with an unusual talent in the larger rise and fall story of the 1970's porn industry. The details and depth of the characters and setting are mesmerizing. The narrative structure is complicated but it carries the sense of inevitability that is the hallmark of a great story. And the camerawork is simply dazzling. The film creates a completely believable and engrossing world and makes us sympathize with characters we might previously have dismissed or been disturbed by. It is a great movie about people who make terrible movies, a magnificently acted film about awful actors. And that is just one of the dualities that make the film so richly rewarding.

Because of the movie's setting and its explicit sex, violence, language, and drug use, it is not for all audiences. But those who are willing to enter into its world will find that it is an enthralling story, brilliantly told, with early performances from actors who would go on to help define the decade, and with a depth that rewards repeated viewing.

Mark Wahlberg plays Eddie, who takes the name Dirk Diggler when he starts making porn movies directed by Jack Horner (Burt Reynolds). Dirk's exceptional physical attributes and stamina quickly make him a superstar of the genre and very soon he enjoys the attention and parties and all the things he can buy. Anderson shows us that he is also happy because the people he works with give him the acceptance and warmth he never had at home. They are very much a family. Dirk becomes even more successful when he and his friend create a series of porn movies with a spy theme.

And then things change. Video comes in and the entire structure of porn production and distribution changes (as it will again when the Internet becomes publicly available). And Dirk finds that getting older and years of drug use make him less fit for performing in the movies he makes.

I am a big fan of the *Save the Cat* screenwriting books by Blake Snyder, not because I want to write a screenplay but because he is one of the best at explaining story structure, the different pieces and how they work (or do not work) together. One idea I learned from him is the way that in many movies first the magic works and then it doesn't. You can see that quite literally in films like "Bruce Almighty," a story about a man played by Jim Carrey who is temporarily granted God's powers. As Snyder says, that leads to "fun and games" and "the promise of the premise" as we enjoy Bruce's petty, guilt-free, self-centered spree that ranges from revenge on his office rival to increasing the size of his girlfriend's breasts. In another Carrey film, "Yes Man," he plays a character who decides to say yes to everything. In both films, it is a lot of fun to see the characters experience a kind of liberation, but inevitably there comes a moment when it stops working and our hero must confront his failings and find (or not find) a greater strength, courage, and resolve than he has ever had before.

The "magic works and then it doesn't" theme works well in drama, too, and "Boogie Nights," like all rise and fall films, is a good example. It is exhilarating to see Dirk's success and Anderson's montage sequence is superbly edited, each element a gem, with, as throughout the movie, perfectly matched to the outstanding soundtrack. But then the magic stops working, and it is devastating.

The moment: Early in the film, Eddie attends a pool party at Jack's house and it is like a master class in using a camera to tell a story. To introduce both Eddie and the audience to the many characters who will become his new family, Anderson uses a five-minute tracking shot, meaning that one unbroken shot takes us all around the party and then dives into the pool. This continuity, in contrast to the usual mosaic mix of long shots and close-ups, makes it seem more direct, more connected, unbroken. Anderson and cinematographer Robert Elswit choreograph the movement of the camera to convey an enormous amount of information. But it also conveys a mood of openness and possibility and pleasure. Later in the film, at another party, there is another long tracking shot but everything is opposite. It is night, not day. It is winter, not summer. It is indoors, not outdoors, and the feeling is physically and emotionally claustrophobic. And the conclusion is horrific, tragic, fatal; instead of opening up it is a closing off of everything. This mirror image adds to the impact of the scene and to our understanding that this is a film in which every decision is carefully considered and brilliantly executed.

More amazing tracking shots:

"Goodfellas"

"Atonement"

"Touch of Evil"

"Children of Men"

"Rope"

23

BOYS ON THE SIDE
(1995)

Bringing the Parties to the Same Page

The movie: Every so often a movie I don't care for much the first time around blooms a bit more on a second and third viewing. They tend to be films where the plot is not very good and once I have let go of trying to make that work I can focus more on the individual scenes, the performances, the chemistry between the actors, and the movie's other strengths. "Boys on the Side" qualifies in all of those categories.

It has the oldest plot of all, the road trip with characters who have to get to know each other as they navigate a journey. That one goes back to The Odyssey and has formed the basis for everything from "The Wizard of Oz" to "Lawrence of Arabia,"and "Lord of the Rings."

Jane, a singer (Whoopi Goldberg) and Robin, a realtor (Mary-Louise Parker), set off on a car trip from New York to California. They meet via ad and appear to have nothing in common. At first, Jane turns Robin down because she does not think she can handle a cross-country car trip with "the whitest woman on the face of the earth." But she has no alternative, so in spite of Robin's affection for the Carpenters, they set off. Along they way they pick up Jane's friend Holly (Drew Barrymore) and there are the usual complications and revelations, joys and sorrows.

The story is not the movie's strong point. What does work is the way this movie gets the way women, even the ones who think they have nothing in common, even the ones who keep very big secrets from each other, can form a bond that encompasses painting their toenails, singing in the car, and protecting each other from some very big threats. Some of the best parts of the movie do not make much sense in terms of a plot but resonate emotionally, as when a few months after the three women stop in Arizona there is a surprise birthday party for Jane with an entire community of devoted friends who act as though they have known her for years -- with the Indigo Girls performing.

Director Herb Ross always worked exceptionally well with actresses ("Steel Magnolias," "The Turning Point"). And the movie gets a boost from a wonderful soundtrack of great women singers including Bonnie Raitt, Annie Lennox, Joan Armatrading, Sheryl Crow, and Stevie Nicks.

The moment: In a road trip movie, there are always a series of revelations when the initially indifferent or antagonistic travelers discover each other's unexpected depth and ability. On the second day of the trip, Jane does not really listen when Robin tells her that as a realtor she has learned about "sizing up situations, handling people, getting what you want from them without them really knowing." But it comes in very handy later that day when they stop in Pittsburgh to see Jane's friend Holly (Drew Barrymore). Holly is in the midst of a fight with her violent drug-dealer boyfriend, who throws her at a wall and punches Jane.

Robin comes in with her best brisk commercial manner and talks to Nick as though he as just asked for a break on closing costs. "My hunch is our two positions might be a lot closer than you think," she tells him, and as he looks on, bewildered, she says confidently to Jane and Holly, "Let me close this." She crisply resolves the issue and then, when things spiral completely out of control, she maintains her cool, telling Nick, "You've got some real likeability issues," and getting everyone out the door. Like Jane, we look at Robin with new interest and begin to think that this journey may be worth taking after all.

More road trip movies:

"Midnight Run"

"The Sure Thing"

"The African Queen"

"Planes, Trains & Automobiles"

"Thelma & Louise"

"It Happened One Night"

§ § §

24

Casa De Los Babys
(2003)

Snow Day Soliloquy

The movie: Writer-director John Sayles makes movies about complicated people in complicated situations. At times, he can focus too much on the latter and come across as preachy, but when he makes the characters the center of the story, his movies are powerful and moving.

The first film he directed was "Return of the Secaucus Seven," a look at a reunion of a group of college friends that pre-dated the more commercial "The Big Chill." (And it was the film debut of actor David Strathairn.) Until the political metaphors overwhelm the story at the end, "Lone Star" is an ambitious drama about race and the impact of the past on future generations. There are a couple of extraordinary scenes, one where an officer played by Joe Morton interviews a young soldier who is in trouble and another when Chris Cooper, who plays a Texas sheriff, visits his ex-wife, played by Frances McDormand. It is one of the best-ever onscreen portrayals of mental illness and marital breakdown. We can understand everything that happened between them and how Cooper's character feels about it as she tells him about the college football team.

The tagline for Sayles' "Casa De Los Babys" is "Six Women. One Dream." Six women from very different backgrounds have traveled to an unidentified Spanish-speaking country with the hope of adopting a child. Sayles is candid but sympathetic in portraying the hopes and fears of the women who want babies and the women who give up babies for adoption.

The moment: Eileen (Susan Lynch of "Waking Ned Devine") describes her dream of the simplest of motherhood pleasures, waking up one morning to discover it is a snow day. You can tell by the way she has thought out every detail down to the marshmallows in the hot cocoa and the way her daughter will have to have some soup before eating French fries just how deeply she wants to be a mother and how much love she is aching to give.

> *It's a day when there's no school. It's a snow day. And I let her sleep late. And she's little, but she's old enough to go to school. She's third grade, maybe. And I let her sleep late. I come in, and she's this little, warm bump in the bed. And I say, "Darling, it's a snow day. I'm gonna let you sleep." You enjoy it more if you know you're getting extra, that usually you'd be up and brushing your teeth. Finally, she gets up and she comes out in her pajamas, and I make her cocoa with...you know those little marshmallows on the top? And then we talk about what we're gonna do that day. And you can hear the snow shovels outside crunching. The plows rumble by every once in a while, scraping the streets, and it's still falling, so it stays clean on top of everything, white. Then I get her dressed... all the layers. Although now it's a lot less with the polar fleece. And she can do most of it herself, but you help because it's a pleasure. Her arm on your neck while she balances to put her boots on. No thought of it. You're just an extension of her body. We go to the Common, or we go way out to Jamaica Pond, depending on the weather. And she's just bold enough to skid out away from me a little bit. Shaky, but she keeps looking back to see if I'm watching her. She always comes back to lean on me and rest.*

And there's zillions of kids, and they're all ages. They're zipping around and that makes her really excited, but mostly, she just wants to be with me. Just the two of us. And then later, when I take her to Shakey's or Ground Round, whatever seems like a big treat to her, and I let her order french fries, as long as she has some of my soup, too, and she tells me stories about her classmates, or she tells me stories that she's made up, or...whatever. We sit and we talk in the booth. And we're surrounded by other mothers and their kids.

It is an exquisitely speech that makes us feel that moment and want it for her as much as she does.

More movies about adoption:

"The Big City"

"Juno"

"Sentimental Journey"

"Losing Isaiah"

"Room for One More"

§ § §

25

THE CHALK GARDEN
(1964)

The Job Interview

The movie: Two of Enid Bagnold's works were adapted for films and it is fascinating to compare them, as they hardly seem to have come from the same planet, much less the same author. While both are stories about young girls, one is "National Velvet," the warm-hearted classic based on Bagnold's novel about a horse-loving girl in an idealized small village, and the less-often remembered other is "The Chalk Garden," based on her play about a troubled girl who lives with her eccentric grandmother and has a governess with a dark secret.

The play premiered on Broadway in 1955 and reflected a mid-century straddling of genres. Its tone and setting recalled the classical drawing room works of the first half of the 20th century but its themes reflected the increased frankness of the post-WWII era. Nine years later, the movie version would have to hint at some of the more disturbing elements of the story because more explicit material would not be seen in films until the late 1960's, but that is an advantage, leaving room for interpretation and ambiguity.

Laurel, the teenager, is played by Hayley Mills in a major departure from her roles as America's sweetheart in Disney films like "Pollyanna," "The Parent Trap," "That Darn Cat," and "Summer Magic." In this film she appears with her father, the distinguished British actor John Mills (an Oscar-winner for "Ryan's Daughter"), who plays Maitland, the manservant.

Laurel feels abandoned by her mother, who has recently

remarried. She had a disturbing experience that is not spelled out explicitly in the film, but in the play it is made clear that she was "violated" at age 12.

She is angry and hurt and so she likes to shock and hurt others. She also likes to start fires. Her grandmother thinks that the best way to handle this is to order the servants to construct bonfires for her to light. Laurel is obsessed with true crime stories, which she discusses at length with Maitland.

The moment: The opening scene brings us into the story immediately as Laurel's grandmother, Mrs. St. Maugham (an imperious Dame Edith Evans) interviews an applicant for the position of governess, Miss Madrigal (Deborah Kerr). It is a bracingly direct exchange between two strong and determined souls who have each survived a great deal. Miss Madrigal is vague about her past and has no references. Mrs. St. Maugham would normally dismiss her immediately. But she needs someone for Laurel. And Miss Madrigal is knowledgeable about the one thing Mrs. St. Maugham cares about almost as much as she cares for Laurel, her garden. The earth in that part of the country is chalky and inhospitable for flowers. Miss Madrigal knows how to enrich the soil.

Yes, this is a metaphor.

Director Ronald Neame ("The Prime of Miss Jean Brodie") assembled a superb cast. While the film is uneven and dated, it is a pleasure to watch them, especially Dame Edith, who shows us that Mrs. St. Maugham, despite her resolve, is frantic with worry. While she stoutly defends Laurel's behavior, claiming that like she is like cracked porcelain, "marred, in some marvelous way for the better!" we see that she feels helpless and that the girl will suffer terribly if she does not reconcile with her own mother. Her fierceness and desperation as she tries to convince herself that Laurel can survive in her emotional chalk garden is heart-wrenching.

More Deborah Kerr as a teacher:

"The King and I"

"The Innocents"

"Tea and Sympathy" (she was a teacher's wife but had important interactions with the students)

"An Affair to Remember" (briefly, in the movie's most superfluous scene)

§ § §

26

Charlie Wilson's War
(2007)

The Scotch Scene

The movie: Who would expect, in the middle of a fact-based Washington political drama about politics, war, national security, and money, a brilliantly staged comic scene with the precision timing of a farce by Georges Feydeau or Alan Ayckbourn? And it is from screenwriter Aaron Sorkin ("The West Wing," "The Social Network"), known for dialog that is intricate, dense, sophisticated, and witty but not for physical comedy. Yet that is one element of a screenplay that is a masterpiece of economy of story-telling and of tone that is as bright as a comedy and as compelling as a drama.

Charlie Wilson (Tom Hanks) is a genial Democratic Congressman from Texas, less open about his strengths (intelligence, expertise, and in some categories, integrity) than he is about his weaknesses, which can be broadly characterized as wine, women, and similar pleasures. When invited onto the Ethics subcommittee, he replies genially, "Well, Jesus, Donnelly. Everyone in town knows I'm on the other side of that issue."

Wilson has a secure seat in Congress and has the luxury of voting his conscience. A news report about refugees feeling Soviet-occupied Afghanistan prompted him to push for increased US support for the Afghanis who were fighting the Soviets. He asks for a briefing from the CIA and the man who arrives in

his Capitol Hill office is Gust Avrakotos (Philip Seymour

Hoffman). Like Wilson, he is an outspoken outsider easily underestimated. Avrakotos brings Wilson a bottle of his favorite Scotch, festooned with a jaunty bow. As they warily get acquainted, there is an interruption by one of the many stunningly beautiful women in Wilson's office known throughout Washington as "Charlie's Angels."

The moment: It seems that Wilson is being investigated for drug use. The staff is instantly on top of it, expertly evaluating the potential harm and composing a statement perfectly balanced between respect for the legal system and dignified incredulousness at the pointlessness of this effort. In a perfectly choreographed series of entrances and exits, Avrakotos and the staffers pop in and out of Wilson's office until a statement is approved and Avrakotos returns with some advice on handling the investigation.

> *Charlie Wilson: Were you standing at the goddamn door listening to me? How could you even - That is a thick door! You stood there and you listened to me?*
>
> *Gust Avrakotos: I didn't stand at the door. Don't be an idiot. I bugged the Scotch bottle.*
>
> *Charlie Wilson: What!*
>
> *Gust Avrakotos: It's got a little transmitter on it, I've got a little thing in my ear, get past it.*

The scene is as brilliantly timed and as hilarious as the Marx Brothers' stateroom scene in "Night at the Opera," and yet it is utterly in keeping with the high-gloss, sophisticated intelligence of the film, giving us a chance to understand the characters and the way they handle crisis as they learn about each other.

More movies about politicians with moral dilemmas:

"All the King's Men"

"The Seduction of Joe Tynan"

"The Great McGinty"

"Alias Nick Beal"

§ § §

27

COLD SOULS
(2009)

Paul Giamatti Looks into His Soul and it Seems to be a Chickpea

The movie: One of the cleverest movies of the last decade is writer-director Sophie Barthes' provocative story of an actor named Paul Giamatti (played by real life actor Paul Giamatti) who thinks that his struggle to play Anton Chekhov's Uncle Vanya on stage will be easier if he takes advantage of a new service he read about in the New Yorker that puts souls in storage. Like "Eternal Sunshine of the Spotless Mind," this is a rare film that truly explores the promise of its premise, and each successive development is fascinatingly mapped out and disarmingly underplayed.

Giamatti (the real life performer) has quite a challenge. Not only does he have to play a version of himself with and without his original soul, he has to play himself as the temporary repository of a soul of Russian poet whose story turns out to be very different from what he had in mind. And he has to rehearse Uncle Vanya in all three modes.

In an interview, Barthes told me that the Vanya scenes were the toughest challenge of the film for her and for Giamatti. "He doesn't like rehearsal much. He is very intuitive. But when it came time to do it badly, for those we took time and rehearsed them. I said, 'Let's not make it robotic, but let's be the opposite of whatever is called for. Confidence is something Vanya doesn't have, so show confidence. Take directions very literally.'" Some of the outtakes with his other approaches are on the DVD, including a sort of William Shatner version.

The story has elements of "Being John Malkovich" or "Stranger Than Fiction," engaging playfully but whole-heartedly with meta-existential issues. It has an appealing story and unexpected and interesting characters, including a Russian mobster and his starlet wife and the upbeat director of the storage business (David Strathairn in a rare comic role). The look of the film is inventive as well. The soul storage facility and the soul removal machines - the sleek upscale one in New York and the black market version in Russia - are witty but believable. It is very funny when Giamatti (the character) finds that while most other souls are intriguingly cloud-like, his looks exactly like a chickpea.

The moment: Giamatti resists looking into his own soul until he is trying to get it back and he must reconnect with it before it will work. He puts on the special goggles, and suddenly he is in an empty white space. A naked toddler walks past him, crying. It is a perfect depiction of that moment, that soul.

Barthes told me that it was a last-minute change. "It is a completely absurd moment and it came about by accident. We had a part in the movie that was a dream I had a long time ago about a baby factory where babies are manufactured. I'm going to put that in another film because it did not work out this time.

When the casting agency came with the babies I was expecting four or five month old babies. But they brought toddlers who could walk, so we gave up on the factory idea and used the set next door with the white space."

More Chekhov:

"Vanya on 42nd Street"

"American Seagull"

§ § §

28

THE COMPANY
(2003)

My Funny Valentine

The movie: Form follows content in Robert Altman's film. As in the lives of the ballet troupe it portrays, it is the dance that takes center stage. The rest of the characters' lives are glimpsed only around the edges. The result is intimate and moving, with dance numbers that are thrillingly filmed and backstage stories that are quietly observed.

This is a ballet film that is not about nutcrackers and tutus. This is a film about people who make the ultimate commitment to art and, especially, it is about the art that they make. Altman was not just showing us dancers here. He was showing us himself.

Neve Campbell (the "Scream" series, "Party of Five"), a former ballet dancer, brought the idea to Altman ("M*A*S*H," "Gosford Park") and she stars as Ry, a member of Chicago's Joffrey Ballet. As the opening credits begin, we hear the usual pre-performance announcements directing the audience to turn off their cell phones and reminding them that photography is prohibited. Then we see a stunning performance of a ballet called "Tensile Involvement," a postmodern angular variation on a maypole dance (or maybe the ribbons on a toe shoe), with dancers interacting with stretched banners and the credits crossing the screen as though they were a part of the choreography.

The off-stage scenes have a loose, documentary feel but they are as meticulously observed and as carefully positioned as a ballerina en pointe. Ry's two sets of parents - divorced mother and father and their new spouses - each bring flowers to her performance. When she hands them back for a moment so that she can talk with someone, the two couples wait a beat, look at each other, and then switch flowers. Ry might not know the difference between the two bouquets, but the people who brought them do. Dancers battle the limits of the physical world as they try to transcend their own sometime reluctant bodies as well as the pulls of gravity, and of time. Ry's non-dancer boyfriend (James Franco) shows that he brings the same kind of care, artistry, and precision to his work as a chef that she does to hers.

The rehearsal scenes mix art and drama as the choreographers treat the primary dancers the way sculptors treat clay while the back-up dancers are "marking" the moves off to the side. Dancers matter-of-factly handle injuries, juggle other jobs, and borrow space for their sleeping bags on each other's floors. The company director breezily shmoozes and evades with just about everyone, but when he accepts an award he is bracingly honest about the way he was treated as a young boy who loved dance.

One technical point worth noting is that this is the first

film to use a new post-production process called Darbee Vision, which adds depth and vivid color to video. It is ideally suited for photographing the dance numbers, which are, after all, center stage. They are lovely, even the weird and garish number that looks something like a Chinese New Year parade.

The moment: Two dancers perform an exquisite pas de deux to a melancholy "My Funny Valentine," danced outdoors. A sudden rainstorm begins. The audience puts up umbrellas and the musicians try to keep their sheet music from flying off the music stands. The techies and ballet management try to figure out whether there is danger of an electrical short or standing water on the stage. And the dance continues, the storm around it framing the number so that what we see is a portrait of lovers so enthralled by each other that even a raging storm could not disrupt their dance.

More ballet on film:

"The Turning Point"

"The Red Shoes"

"Mao's Last Dancer"

§ § §

29

The Court Jester
(1957)

The Sword Fight

The movie: "Life could not better be" than the pure cinematic joy of this movie from the first frame to the last. Danny Kaye has his best role as Hawkins, a follower of the Black Fox, a Robin Hood-style rebel who hopes to put the infant royal heir on the throne in place of the usurper.

Hawkins is assigned to entertain the troops and watch over the baby, who has the royal birthmark on his rear. He wishes for more exciting assignments like those given to Jean (Glynis Johns), a smart, courageous, and tough Captain of the rebel forces. Hawkins loves her but has not been able to tell her.

Hawkins finally gets his chance for a more active role when he gets to disguise himself as Giacomo, the King's new jester, to get access to the palace. He does not know that the real Giacomo is also undercover - in reality, he is an assassin brought in to murder the usurper in favor of another usurper, Sir Ravenhurst (go-to bad guy who is good with a sword Basil Rathbone). Hawkins finds himself in the midst of intrigue, hypnotized into wooing the Princess (Angela Lansbury) by her lady in waiting (Mildred Natwick), and ordered by Sir Ravenhurst to kill those who stand between him and the throne.

Every scene in this film is a gem. Perhaps the best-remembered is the hilarious exchange about the pellet with the poison and the vessel with the pestle. Just as good is the battle with a huge knight named Sir Griswold, where Hawkins' armor is magnetized by lightning. And it is worth pointing out the scene in which Jean and Hawkins confess their love for one another. He asks shyly if she could love a man who was not a fighter, and she explains that tenderness and kindness are important to her. They are each proud of the other the way they are, almost revolutionary for a movie of that era.

The moment: The sword fight scene with Hawkins and Sir Ravenhurst is a special treat because it is really two sword fights in one. The lady in waiting hypnotizes Hawkins into thinking that he is a master swordsman. While he is under the spell, he fights like one. But a snap of the fingers is the signal to put him into and out of the trance. Just as he is about to deliver the final thrust, Hawkins majestically says, "Your life isn't worth that!" imperiously snapping his fingers. Instantly, he has no idea of how to fight. He flails wildly for a moment until Ravenhurst snaps his fingers, and they're off again.

It is a spectacular sword fight when Hawkins is under the spell and becomes a master swordsman. He taunts

Ravenhurst by pouring and drinking a goblet of water while he slashes away. And it is simply masterful when Hawkins has no skills at all, and a tribute to Rathbone's real-life championship fencing skills that he and Kaye make his clumsiest thrusts look supremely lucky.

More from Danny Kaye:

"White Christmas"

"Merry Andrew"

"Up in Arms"

More from Basil Rathbone:

"The Adventures of Robin Hood"

"The Adventures of Sherlock Holmes"

"The Mark of Zorro"

§ § §

30

Crash
(2005)

Bedtime Story

The movie: This surprise Best Picture Oscar winner is nonetheless underrated, with many people feeling that it unjustly won over "Brokeback Mountain" due to homophobia. But in its own way, "Crash" engages with issues as incendiary and with as much honesty and compassion as "Brokeback Mountain" and with more complexity in its script and performances than it is given credit for.

"Crash" takes place in a world where everyone is angry. Everyone is scared. They all feel that something that belongs to them has been taken away and they don't know how to get it back. And they say so. It is an ensemble film with several intersecting stories, all of them about people who can't quite seem to understand how things turned out the way they did or how they themselves turned out the way they did. Most of them find out, in the course of the movie, that they are capable of more -- or less -- than they thought they were.

It almost seems that the drinking water in Los Angeles has been spiked with some mild de-inhibitor that makes people say what they are thinking. In this film, everyone says the most horrifyingly virulent things to everyone else: family members, people in business, employees, and strangers, reflecting a range of prejudice on the basis of class, gender, and, above all, race. These comments are sometimes made angrily, sometimes carelessly or thoughtlessly, but often, and more unsettlingly, matter-of-factly.

The movie is intricately constructed, going back and forth between the characters and back and forth in time. There are glimpses of moments that create a mosaic in which we see the pattern before the characters do. The movie has big shocks but it also has small glimpses and moments of great subtlety. A black woman looks at her white boss while he talks to his wife on a cell phone and we can tell there is more to their relationship than we have been told. The daughter of immigrants we have only seen in one context shows up in another and we see that her professional life is very different from what we might have imagined, reminding us that racism may be inextricably intertwined with America, but so is opportunity.

The brilliance of the movie is the way it makes each character both symbol and individual. As a whole, the cast is neatly aligned along a continuum of prejudice, and yet each character is complete and complex and real. Just when we think we know who they are, they surprise us. We find ourselves sympathetic to those we thought we hated and disturbed by those we thought we understood. Just when we think we know what bigotry is, it, too, surprises us by being more about fear and loss and feeling powerless than about hatred and ignorance. The characters confront their assumptions about each other and they make us confront our own about them and about ourselves.

The moment: One of the tenderest father-daughter scenes ever filmed is the set-up for an explosive emotional pay-off later on. Michael Peña plays Daniel, a locksmith who is doing his best to keep his young daughter safe. She is frightened by hearing a gunshot. He tells her they are in a safer neighborhood than they were before, but she is still upset about the time a bullet came through her window. So he tells her a story about the time he saw a fairy.

She had these little stubby wings, like she could've glued them on, you know, like I'm gonna believe she's a fairy. So she said, "I'll prove it." So she reaches into her backpack and pulls out this invisible cloak and she ties it around my neck. And she tells me that it's impenetrable. You know what impenetrable means? It means nothing can go through it. No bullets, nothing. She told me that if I wore it, nothing would hurt me. And I did. And my whole life, I never got shot, stabbed, nothing. I mean, how weird is that? Only she tells me I'm supposed to give it to my daughter on her sixth birthday. And I forgot....If you want I can take it off and tie it around your shoulders, 'cause she showed me how to do that.

He unties the invisible cloak and puts it around her shoulders. "You feel anything?" She shakes her head. "Good, then it's just right....Leave it on all the time. 'Til you grow up and have a daughter and she turns six. Then you give it to her, okay?

His daughter is comforted. And for a moment, with this lovely reminder that in the midst of all of the terrible fear and anger there is still sweetness and care for the vulnerable, and hope, so are we.

More from Michael Peña:

"World Trade Center"

"The Lincoln Lawyer"

"Lions for Lambs"

"Tower Heist"

§ § §

31

DIE HARD
(1988)

Alan Rickman Makes a Fast Switch

The movie: Writer Rodrick Thorp saw the movie, "The Towering Inferno," and that night he dreamed of a man being chased through an office building by men with guns. He turned that idea into a sequel to his book, *The Detective* (made into a movie by that name starring Frank Sinatra). And that book, which he called *Nothing Lasts Forever* was adapted for one of the most enduringly popular action films of all time, "Die Hard," starring Bruce Willis.

It is Christmas. New York City cop John McLane (Willis) is on his way to see his estranged wife at her new office in the Nakatomi building, a skyscraper in LA. But the building is taken over by Hans Gruber (Alan Rickman in his first feature film) who wants the authorities to think he is a terrorist. That is a diversion -- he is just after money in the form of bearer bonds. Gruber has figured everything out based on standard police procedures. But McLane is anything but standard. He hides out in the building and defeats Gruber's men one by one as they come after him, despite a lot of interference from well-meaning cops, civilians, and a television reporter and with some help from a good-hearted local police officer.

Willis is ideally cast as a wise-ass cop who does not play by the rules. His wife (Bonnie Bedelia) sees how angry one of the bad guys is and instantly knows her husband is still alive: "Only John can drive someone that crazy." The script, largely based on Thorp's book, is clever and exciting. But one of the best plot turns was impromptu, inspired by some off-screen fooling around.

Rickman, now best known as "Harry Potter's" Severus Snape, was born in London and is a classically trained actor. This is a rare instance where a newcomer playing the villain takes full advantage of the audience's unfamiliarity to keep surprising us. (Another good example is Edward Norton, who was nominated for an Oscar for his first performance in "Primal Fear.")

The moment: As Gruber, Rickman speaks with a German accent. For most of the movie, while we see Gruber, his only contact with McLane is his voice, via the walkie-talkie and intercom system.

Then the two men see each other for the first time and we expect a confrontation. But Rickman was showing off his impeccable American accent between scenes and director John McTiernan realized that this presented a great opportunity for a twist.

McLane rushes in and sees a man who starts talking to him with a perfect American accent. He seamlessly eases straight into another accent and another persona. As the fi-

nal version of the shooting script puts it, "The transformation in his expression and bearing are mind-boggling." Instead of the icy German barking orders, he is immediately a completely convincing terrified American, begging McLane not to shoot. We know it is Gruber, but McLane doesn't.

Whether McLane is convinced or not is for us to discover. But at that moment, Rickman is so persuasive, even some audience members may be confused.

More from Rickman:

"Truly Madly Deeply"

"Something the Lord Made"

"Dogma"

"Sense and Sensibility"

§ § §

32

DINER
(1982)

The Guys Stop forSomething to Eat

The movie: Writer-director Barry Levinson based "Diner" on his own experiences growing up in Baltimore in the late 1950's. It is a very specific but universal coming-of-age story of a group of young men who are happiest hanging out in their usual booth, making idiotic bets, trading insults, challenging each other on trivia, and enjoying the feeling of being completely accepted and understood. In the rest of the world, girls are mysterious and scary and families make unpleasant demands. But at the diner, everything seems familiar and they feel at home and unconditionally accepted.

It is almost New Year's Eve and the end of the decade. As momentous, Eddie (Steve Guttenberg) is about to become the second of the five to get married -- if his fiancée can pass a test of football knowledge that he insists on as a prerequisite. He has also demanded "Colts colors" for the wedding theme.

The prospective groom finally and clumsily reveals his fears that marriage is scary to Shrevie (Daniel Stern), the other married member of the group (whose relationship is, if not scary, filled with misunderstandings and isolation). "We'll always have the diner," is the most reassuring thing Shrevie can say, and somehow that is enough.

All of the group are lost everywhere but the diner. Eddie is terrified of marriage. Shrevie is finding that now that the wedding is over and it is no longer necessary to make elaborate logistical arrangements to have sex he and his wife have nothing to say to one another and she does not honor his elaborate LP filing system or extensive mastery of arcane detail. In one of the most plaintive complaints ever filmed, he says desperately to her, "You never ask me what's on the flip-side!"

Boogie (Mickey Rourke) is deeply in debt over gambling losses and mesmerized by the unattainable vision of wealthy blonde girl galloping on her horse. Fenwick (Kevin Bacon) is about to come to the end of his trust fund and has no prospects for taking care of himself. And Billy (Timothy Daly), in most ways the one who has made the most progress toward adulthood, loves a girl who will not commit to him, even though she is pregnant with his child.

At this writing, the movie is being adapted for a Broadway musical by Levinson and rock star Sheryl Crow.

The moment: This movie is filled with great moments, including an outlandish (and unsuitable for family viewing) bet involving popcorn in a movie theater, a trip to a sleazy bar, the hilarious football quiz (the bride is never seen), and the Colts colors wedding. But the scenes that really tell the story of the movie are, appropriately, the ones in the diner. Levinson threw his young cast together and waited to shoot those scenes until the end of the filming so they would have time to develop natural rhythms, with some of the dialog improvised. The jockeying over which is better, Mathis or Sinatra is every irresistibly idiotic but somehow riveting and reassuring battle over the minutia that defines us and our friendships forever.

More from Barry Levinson:

"Avalon"

"Rain Man"

"Good Morning, Vietnam"

33

Dirty Rotten Scoundrels (1988)

Ruprecht

The movie: Dale Launer wrote three of the freshest and smartest comedies of the late 1980's and early 1990's, the original scripts "My Cousin Vinny" and "Ruthless People" and a remake that is a big improvement on the original, "Dirty Rotten Scoundrels." It was based on the 1964 "Bedtime Story," starring Marlon Brando and David Niven as continental con men with very different styles who competed with each other to determine who would get the run of the Riviera.

The story of the remake deserves a movie of its own. Launer wrote,

> I saw it in the late '60's on TV when I was home from school. Years later I became a screenwriter and got a call from David Bowie's production company. He and Mick Jagger wanted to do a movie together and hoped I would write it. I suggested doing a remake of "Bedtime Story" with Bowie as Lawrence Jamison and Mick as Freddy. They were both interested, the studio (UA) was interested, but the movie had been made at Universal and there was no way they could get the rights. A number of other studios were interested, but couldn't wrestle the right away from Universal. Turns out no one had bothered to do a copyright search. I did. Turns out the rights had reverted back to the original writer/producer Stanley Shapiro. We met at the Pink Turtle (a coffee shop at what was the Beverly Wilshire) and did a deal on a

napkin.

The original title was "King of Hill." Since Stanley was the man behind the Doris Day/Rock Hudson/Cary Grant movies -- he decided to write (with Maurice Richlin - who went on to pen the original "Pink Panther") a movie where Cary Grant and Rock Hudson would compete for Doris Day. Apparently, Cary had asked Rock to do a movie with him, but Rock had turned him down. So Cary didn't want to do a movie with Rock. And Doris wouldn't do the movie without the both of them. Hence it was re-cast with Niven, Brando and Shirley Jones.

Stanley said this movie didn't do all that well in its original run. He felt that the movie fell flat in the south because of Brando championing civil rights. Though I do prefer my ending, this is nevertheless a very charming movie. Which is why I tried to preserve as much as the original as possible.

Hey, if ain't broke, don't fix it. And certainly don't change it.

Launer is too modest. His version is far better. It inspired a Broadway musical in 2005.

Michael Caine plays the elegant Lawrence Jamieson, who maintains his magnificent home on the ocean by romancing wealthy women who come to the Riviera on vacation. He tells them that he is royalty in exile and cannot marry them because all of his efforts must go to the freedom fighters in his home country. They are proud to hand over generous contributions and go back home knowing that they have been loved by a prince and supported his cause.

Steve Martin is Freddy Benson, whose con man stories are less graceful and more maudlin. His specialty is the more short-term, lower yield con, a meal here, a couple of hundred dollars there. When he arrives in the Riviera, he offends Lawrence's sense of propriety and presents a risk of making the community more aware of potential fraud. Lawrence wants him to leave. Freddy wants to stay. Lawrence agrees to take Freddy on as an apprentice and it works for a while. But when Freddy wants to strike out on his own, they make a bet. They will both go after the same mark, and whoever gets her money can stay.

Professor of film-turned lawyer Alan Dale, author of the brilliant book about slapstick, *Comedy is a Man in Trouble*, has an superb list of what matters in movies:

1. structure
2. structure
3. structure
4. virtuosity
5. sex
6. violence
7. music
8. [reserved]
9. [reserved]
10. ideas

Many writers can come up with funny situations and laugh lines, but Launer is a master of all that and of structure as well. The characters and witty dialog and pretty settings are very amusing the first time through. But all three of these films work on second, third, and even tenth viewings because they are marvelously constructed so that the comic developments are earned and even the surprises feel organic and deliciously inevitable.

The moment: The series of scenes showing how Lawrence both teaches Freddy how to be a con man and finds a way to humiliate him in their team-ups is flat-out hilarious because it is designed to both separate wealthy ladies from their money and to humiliate Freddy and does both very well. Freddy is assigned the

role of "Ruprecht," the prince's brother, deranged apparently as the result of generations of inbreeding. His job is to be so appalling that the women who think they will be marrying a prince will be glad to back out and provide a nice financial going-away gift. Martin is in his element and the interplay between his efforts to come up with the most repellent behavior possible and Caine's effortless urbanity furthers the sense of competition between them as it leaves the audience helpless with laughter.

More from Dale Launer:

"My Cousin Vinny"

"Ruthless People"

§ § §

34

Divorce American Style
(1967)

The Joint Custody Roundelay

The movie: Norman Lear is best known for iconic television comedies like "All in the Family," "Maude," "The Jeffersons," "Sanford and Son," and "One Day at a Time." But this neglected gem is one of his best and most significant works, a brilliantly caustic and sharply observed comedy about the dissatisfactions of middle class suburban life.

This is what I call a "full catastrophe" movie, from the reply in "Zorba the Greek," when the title character is asked if he is married. "I'm a man, so I married," he responds. "Wife, children, house, everything. The full catastrophe." The counterpoint to all of the aspirational "happily ever after" movies that define success as it is displayed in glossy magazine ads, the comedies from this era tend to hold up better than the dramas ("Strangers When We Meet," "The Man in the Gray Flannel Suit"). The kids of this era would grow up and give their own take in even more acerbic films like "The Ice Storm."

"That's my father's hand, hanging out of my sleeve," says Richard Harmon (Dick Van Dyke), looking despondently down at his hand with the wedding ring as he sits at a bar with his best friend, unhappy about a fight with his wife Barbara (Debbie Reynolds). Neither Richard nor Barbara can tell exactly why they feel so empty when they have achieved everything they thought they wanted. He has a successful career and they have children and a beautiful home. But both feel a longing they cannot describe. Both are hurt that each can't seem to make the other happy. They fall into a process that has them on the way to a divorce without either really knowing how they got there.

The film is a series of painful – and hilarious -- scenes as Richard finds himself living on $87.30 a week while Barbara gets the rest of his income in alimony and child support. While their lawyers chat about mutual acquaintances and make a date to play golf, Richard and Barbara argue about dividing their property. Richard meets another divorced dad, Nelson Downes (a wry Jason Robards), who goes out every weekend trolling for someone to marry his ex (Jean Simmons) so that he can stop paying alimony and get married to his pregnant girlfriend, "Incidentally letting some poor schnook in Bakersfield off the hook," her first husband.

In some ways, the film is a time capsule from an era that seems very far away. The characters constantly talk about how much things cost or how much they make and you would have to add a zero or two to bring them in line with today's figures. No-fault divorce and working women have changed the financial and emotional dynamics of divorce. But the satiric bite and the wrenching feelings for both the adults and children are still valid.

The moment: "We're going to pick up the two kids from my second marriage now. These two are from my first," says Barbara's date (Tom Bosley). It is Sunday and he is on his way to his ex-wife's house. Two other men arrive for various other pick-ups and there is a scramble for the kids, several of whom cannot quite remember which family they are supposed to be with. "I want to go with Daddy!" "No, today you go with me." "No, you're not with this brother; you're with the other brother!" "It's Sunday, remember? Today you go with Uncle Daddy." The daddies chase after the kids like clumsy cowboys trying to catch stray calves. And everyone races off, leaving one little girl clutching her blanket behind until a car returns to scoop her up.

More movies about divorce:

"Bye Bye Love"

"Kramer vs. Kramer"

"Starting Over"

"Waiting to Exhale"

"An Unmarried Woman"

"Mrs. Doubtfire"

"It's Complicated"

§ § §

35

Dog Day Afternoon
(1975)

Sal Picks Wyoming

The movie: In 1972, John Wojtowicz and his accomplice Sal Naturile held seven Chase Manhattan bank employees on East Third Street and Avenue P in Brooklyn hostage for 14 hours. The robbers kept law enforcement in a standoff while they ordered pizza. By the time word got out that the motive for the robbery was raising money for Wojtowicz's boyfriend to get a sex-change operation, New Yorkers began to support the robbers as anti-heroes. Naturile was killed by the FBI and Wojtowicz was arrested and sentenced to 20 years in prison. He never ended up taking any money from the bank, but he used the $7500 he got for selling the story to the movies to pay for his boyfriend's sexual reassignment surgery. The story became "Dog Day Afternoon," directed by Sidney Lumet and starring Al Pacino, with an Oscar-winning screenplay by Frank Pierson.

The same year this film was released, the New York Daily News ran its famous headline about the President's refusal to provide a federal bail-out: "Ford to New York: Drop Dead." Lumet and Pierson made the robbery emblem and metaphor for the frustration and urban decay of the near-bankrupt New York of the 1970's.

Pacino is electrifying as Sonny Wortzik (the Wojtowicz character) and his phone call with his boyfriend, Leon (Chris Sarandon), mostly improvised by the two actors, is like a perfect little movie of its own. It is heart-wrenching, hilarious, and tragic, and yet the devotion between them provides a surprising moment of sanity and connection in the middle of a mad, broken world.

Sal is played by John Cazale, an actor who died at 42. He made only five films but every one of them was nominated for a Best Picture Oscar. He played Fredo in the first two "Godfather" films and he appeared in "The Conversation" and "The Deer Hunter." A 2009 documentary about him, "I Knew It Was You: Rediscovering John Cazale" is a moving reminder of his talent, dedication, and enduring legacy.

The moment: Sonny is not a criminal mastermind, but he has a lot of heart and feels responsible for taking care of everyone around him, including his wife, his boyfriend, and Sal. Sonny tries to keep Sal focused and reassured by getting him to think about where they go in the plane they have demanded. "Is there any special country you want to go to?" he asks encouragingly. Whatever Sal dreams of, Sonny wants to make it a reality.

Sal thinks for a second, and says, "Wyoming." Sonny says gently, "Wyoming, that's not a country." But Sal's dimness just makes Sonny feel even more responsible for taking care of him. "That's all right, I'm going to take care of it," he says reassuringly. In the middle of a loud, out-of-control event, there is a quiet moment of compassion and loyalty.

More with John Cazale:

"The Godfather"

"The Godfather II"

"The Conversation"

"The Deer Hunter"

36

DRUMLINE
(2002)

"What's the Last Rule in the Rulebook?"

The movie: We first see Devon (Nick Cannon) graduating from high school in Harlem and we learn three things right away. First, when he gives the class musical performance a little extra zing despite the disapproval of his music teacher, we see that he is a very gifted musician who enjoys breaking the rules. Second, we see after the ceremony that his relationship with his mother is warm and close. And third, when he goes to visit the father who abandoned them to tell him that he is proud of himself and the success he achieved without a father, we see that he is tough and principled and has a sure sense of who he is.

All of those qualities will be tested when he becomes a freshman at a historically black Southern college on a music scholarship. He has been recruited to play on the school's marching band. The training sessions are like boot camp and the competition is fierce. And what works with the teenage girls back home does not get him very far down South. Devon has been used to doing things his own way. But now he is a part of something and their motto is "One band. One sound." His instincts are strong and he is willing to work hard but he has a lot to learn about taking responsibility for making sure that everyone looks good. And he has a secret that puts his future in the program at risk.

It is a traditional coming of age story but director Charles Stone III makes it fresh with the benefit of its unusual and striking setting. The precision and artistry of the bands, mostly made up of real-life members of local marching bands, shot and edited with arresting visual flair.

Like the character he plays, Cannon is a performer with enormous appeal and natural ease that comes across as confident but not cocky. His fellow band mates and the pretty philosophy major (Zoe Saldana) and bandleader (Orlando Jones) are skillfully sketched.

The moment: Devon has not had an easy life but he is undisciplined and used to being able to get by on talent and charm. Early in the training, he tries to bluff his way through the answer to a question: "What is the last rule in the rule book?" But the last rule in the rulebook is designed to catch those who try to slide by without reading through to the end: If you can't recite it, you get your head shaved.

At first, Devon refuses to give up his cornrows. But then he accepts it as he does the even harder lessons he has to learn about what "one band, one sound" really means, with gratitude and grace. When the new freshmen arrive, each musician is told why his or her instrument is really the heart of the music. But we never doubt that the real heart is the drumline, and that Devon earns his role as the heart of the band.

More from Orlando Jones:

"The Replacements"

"Bedazzled"

"Liberty Heights"

§ § §

37

Everybody Rides the Carousel (1975)

Trick or Treating

The movie: Faith Hubley described the animated films she made with her husband John as "an odd combination of primitive, childlike, and really sophisticated."

John Hubley worked at Disney on classic animated films like "Snow White," "Bambi," and "Fantasia." But after Frank Lloyd Wright showed him a Russian animated film, "The Tale of the Czar Durandai" directed by Ivan Ivanov-Vano, he was inspired to develop a more impressionistic, improvisational style. Instead of precise images painted on cels, the Hubleys worked with watercolor on paper. They often used recordings of unscripted conversations for the dialog. Voices provided by non-actors like musician Dizzy Gillespie had jazz-infused cadences that gave the films an improvisational, overheard feel. The audio for one of their best films, "Windy Day," was a recording of their daughters talking as they played together, not knowing that anyone was listening.

Hubley left Disney for UA, where he created the character of Mr. Magoo and started his own firm, Storyboard Studios. He and Faith supported themselves by making commercials for products like Maypo cereal and short films for "Sesame Street" and they made an ambitious commitment to release one independent animated movie a year. They won three Oscars for short films and they made this feature-length film inspired by the work of psychologist Erik Erikson.

The self-educated (and self-named) Erikson pioneered

a theory of human psychological development around the search for identity. He saw life as divided into stages, each of which gives us a choice between healthy (strong, curious, independent, loving) and unhealthy (insecure, grasping, isolating) development. The Hubleys created a series of scenes with characters who are faced with these choices.

The moment: Erikson's last stage of choices is "ego integrity vs. despair." As we face the end of our lives, will it be with bitterness and fear or with a sense of satisfaction and generosity?

This is a superb film and its best moments are in expressing this divide. One elderly couple bickers as they go through a cafeteria line. The other waits at home on Halloween for trick-or-treaters to come to the door. Musician Harry Edison and actress Juanita Moore provide the voices for the couple who clearly enjoy each other and the costumes of the children. As the specters of ghosts and skeletons foreshadow what lies ahead in a beautiful match of form and theme, they are able to cherish what they have and what they have had.

More from John and Faith Hubley:

"Windy Day"

"The Hat"

"Moonbird"

§ § §

38

Fade to Black
(2004)

Selling Gangsta Culture

The movie: Jay-Z (born Shawn Corey Carter) has won 13 Grammy awards and sold more than 50 million albums worldwide. He is also a successful producer and entrepreneur, and he is married to the dazzling Beyoncé. This concert film documents what at the time was supposed to be his final album and his final performance, a charity concert at Madison Square Garden. It features appearances by many of the most prominent performers in the hip-hop world, including Ghostface Killah, Lil Kim, P. Diddy, Mary J. Blige, Foxy Brown, Missy Elliot, and the then-future Mrs. Jay-Z, Beyoncé.

It is a fascinating and important film about a brilliant businessman as well as a musician and about the role that hip-hop music plays in our culture, especially the appeal that it has for young people of all races and backgrounds.

The moment: Backstage, aspiring young performers talk about the conflict they feel knowing that in order to be successful they must pander to stereotypes about "gangstas" instead of addressing a wider range of issues or exploring their own experiences and feelings.

Jay-Z begins by saying that he thinks the violence and drug problems of the inner city are not as bad as they were when he was younger and that it takes people speaking out against it to make a difference. But, he says, it is not his style to do so. "You're not that type of rapper," one of his friends agrees. "For two lines out of a 60-minute tape," he says, "for 30 seconds, I felt like saying something, to speak on what's going on in the hood, should I not do that? Should I ignore those feelings?"

Young hip-hop artists who want to be as successful as Jay-Z then talk about their conflicts. "You rapping on shooting and killing people," Jay-Z says to one of them. "They the one who buy it. That's what people want to hear," the other responds. "Truthfully, it's whack. I've been feeling that way, too. I don't be wanting to do that. It seems that sometimes that's all the n*** want to hear." Another one advises him to "be you," asking "Why would you write a rhyme that you don't want to write?" Does he want to write what he feels or what will help his career? He does not think his music will sell if he tries something different, even if it is more honest.

Jay-Z tells the documentary cameraman to focus on him so he can speak directly to us in the audience. "See what you, the public, did to rappers? They scared to be theyselves. N*** don't think that people gonna accept them as theyself."

It is as powerful and telling a moment about art, mortality, culture, and identity as has ever been filmed.

More hip-hop documentaries:

"Tupac: Resurrection"

"Beats, Rhymes & Life: The Travels of A Tribe Called Quest"

"Freestyle: The Art of Rhyme"

"Dave Chapelle's Block Party"

§ § §

39

Father of the Bride (1950)

"Pops" Comforts Kay

The movie: In this era of Bridezillas and entire television series devoted to wedding cakes, we are used to the idea of the chaotic extravaganza surrounding a bride and groom. But in the post-WWII era, when Americans were still getting used to post-war prosperity, Edward Streeter's popular book about Stanley Banks, a father overwhelmed by his daughter's impending nuptials, was a humorously reassuring reminder that peace and plenty had returned.

Vincente Minnelli ("Meet Me in St. Louis," "Gigi") directed the movie adaptation but its enduring appeal is attributable to its stars, the enchantingly beautiful Elizabeth Taylor (age 18 and about to embark on her own wedding, the first of eight) as Kay, and, in the title role, Spencer Tracy. They became very close making this film and the sequel and to the end of their lives she affectionately called him "Pops."

Tracy is superb as the father who struggles to accept that his daughter is grown up – and to try to maintain some control of the budget. It is a completely natural performance, full of heart, and a wonderful opportunity to see what he did best. Tracy and his "Inherit the Wind" co-star Fredric March both played the title roles in "Dr. Jekyll and Mr. Hyde" films, 10 years apart. Both are good but they make a fascinating contrast in approach. March used make-up and prostheses to transform from the doctor into his evil manifestation, but Tracy's transformation is pure acting.

That is because, unlike many actors, Tracy did not like to change his look for a role. He relied on his ability to convey the character's thoughts and emotions. And there is no better example of that than in this film. Tracy plays a man who is struggling to maintain some sense of control in a house where the wedding and its attendant expenditures seem to have taken on a life of their own.

What makes up for the silly struggles over the bills and guest list and the embarrassing encounters with the new in-laws is the way the movie makes the real story his bittersweet sense of loss as his daughter leaves home. "She'll always love us of course, but not in the old way," he thinks. "From now on her love will be handed out like a farmer's wife tossing scraps to the family rooster." In an early scene, Kay is about to go out on a date with her fiancé, Buckley, and Stanley tells her it is chilly and she should wear something warm. She laughs him off but when Buckley arrives and tells her to get a sweater, she meekly agrees. Later, Stanley discovers that his old tuxedo is not only very old but much too small, yet another in a series of painful reminders that he is not what he was and a whole separate set of reminders that he will have to spend more money than he hoped.

The moment: That makes the moment when Stanley does get to provide some advice and support to Kay even more precious. It is also one of the best examples of acting without words ever filmed.

It is almost the day of the wedding when Kay comes home from a date with Buckley distraught and announces that the wedding is off. She goes upstairs and into her bedroom, shutting the door. Stanley tells his wife he will go after her.

He enters Kay's room and sits down near her. Soberly, he reassures her that if she wants to cancel the wedding, he will handle it and asks gently if there's another woman. She says she wishes that was the problem; this is much more serious. Her father looks over at her, devoted and attentive. Finally, she tells him the problem and the contrast between the horror in her voice and the actual source of the problem is very funny and very endearing.

"Nova Scotia."

Yes, Buckley - unforgivably -- booked the honeymoon in Nova Scotia, thinking Kay would find fishing in a rustic cabin a romantic getaway. Spencer Tracy's expression is a masterpiece of acting, a combination of concealed amusement, relief, sympathy, affection, remembrance of a lifetime of Nova Scotia-style misunderstandings of his own, and recognition that his beloved Kay will soon learn that even the happiest of marriages require some adjustment. It is a privileged moment of great sweetness, beautifully expressed.

More movie brides with memorable fathers:

"It Happened One Night"

"The Philadelphia Story"

"My Big Fat Greek Wedding"

"Monsoon Wedding"

§ § §

40

Finding Nemo
(2003)

The Lucky Fin

The movie: Pixar Studios may have the most advanced animation technology in the world, but they never forget what matters most in a movie: story, characters, imagination, and heart. "Finding Nemo" has it all.

It is an epic journey filled with adventure and discovery encompassing the grandest sweep of ocean vastness and the smallest longing of the heart.

Marlin (Albert Brooks) is a fond but nervous and overprotective clown fish with just one child, Nemo. On his first day of school, Nemo swims too far from the others and is captured by a deep-sea diver, a dentist who keeps fish in his office aquarium. Marlin must go literally to the end of the ocean to find his son and bring him home. Meanwhile, Nemo has made some very good friends in the dentist's aquarium, including a tough Tiger Fish (Willem Dafoe) who helps him plan an escape.

And so, in the tradition and spirit of stories from the Odyssey to "The Wizard of Oz," Marlin takes a journey that will introduce him to extraordinary characters and teach him a great deal about the world and even more about himself. He meets up with Dory (Ellen DeGeneres), a cheerful blue tang who has a problem with short-term memory loss. They search for Nemo together, despite stinging jellyfish, exploding mines, and creatures with many, many, many, many teeth.

The film cleverly upends audience expectations about

what and who is scary, though. The shark may have pearly white and very sharp teeth, but he's a vegetarian. Unlike the classical fairy tale (and traditional Disney) bad guys, no one here acts out of jealousy or greed. The closest thing to a villain is a careless 8-year-old.

It is a glorious visual feast. The play of light on the water is breathtaking. The characters imagined by Pixar in their previous film, "Monsters, Inc." were fabulously inventive, but they have nothing on the even more fabulously inventive Mother Nature. This movie will make an ichthyologist out of anyone, because all of the characters are based on real-life ocean species, each one more marvelous than the one before. While preserving their essential "fishy-ness," Pixar and the talented people providing the voices have also made them each wonderfully expressive, and it seems only fair to say that they create performances as full and varied as the best of live action films. But best of all is the way it addresses questions that are literally at the heart of the parent-child relationship. It is a genuine family film, giving everyone in the audience something to relate to and learn from.

The moment: Characters with disabilities in movies tend to suffer from what I call "Smurfette syndrome." Each of the male Smurfs has some personality or profession but Smurfette's only attribute is that she is female. In movies, characters with disabilities are presumed to need no other attributes. And most often their job in the movie is to be saintly by the end, if not all the way through. But Nemo just happens to have an under-developed fin. It does not define him. Marlin does a good job of making Nemo feel confident and unselfconscious. In a very sweet, understated moment early on, they call it his "lucky fin."

But it does make Marlin a little more anxious about protecting Nemo, and it makes Nemo a little more anxious about proving that he can take care of himself. The movie handles Nemo's disability frankly but matter-of-factly, with far more sensitivity, intelligence, and accuracy than all but a few live-action, high-prestige films.

More from Pixar:

"Wall•E"

"A Bug's Life"

"Up"

"The Incredibles"

"Monsters, Inc."

"Brave"

§ § §

41

THE FISHER KING
(1991)

A Waltz in Grand Central Station

The movie: A legend going back to the days of King Arthur tells of a wounded king who cannot meet his responsibilities as a ruler or as the keeper of the Holy Grail. All he can do is fish in the river near his castle and wait for the chosen knight who can heal him. "The Fisher King" is a movie from screenwriter Richard LaGravenese and prodigiously creative director Terry Gilliam about Jack Lucas, a radio host devastated by tragedy (Jeff Bridges) who meets Parry, a mentally ill homeless man obsessed with the legend of the Fisher King (Robin Williams), each in need of healing.

Jack makes an insensitive comment on the air that inspired a listener to commit a mass murder. One of the people killed was Parry's wife. Years later, still devastated, Jack meets Parry and is very taken with Parry's retelling of the fisher kin legend, especially the part where no one can locate the Holy Grail by seeking it. The only one who can find it is the simple boy who wanted to give the thirsty king some water. The movie plays with the themes of the legend. Both Jack and Parry are wounded and unable to function and each is a Fisher King in his own way.

Jack thinks that if he can help Parry it will expiate some of his responsibility for the tragedy. Parry has admired a shy young woman named Lydia (Amanda Plummer) but been unable to talk to her. Jack arranges for them to go on a date and coaches him on how to behave.

Terry Gilliam was the only non-British member of the Monty Python troupe, where he contributed the enchantingly weird paper-cutout animations used as interstitials. He was also a co-writer of some of their material including "The Life of Brian." His wildly imaginative films with striking visuals include classics "Time Bandits" and "Brazil" and some fascinating failures like "The Imaginarium of Doctor Parnassus," with the last performance of Heath Ledger.

One of his most fascinating movies is not by him but about him. "Lost in La Mancha" is a documentary about Gilliam's failed Don Quixote movie project. The parallel between the dreamer who tilts at windmills and the director who tried to mount an adaptation of Cervantes' epic story with additions like a time-traveling advertising executive, is not overlooked.

The moment: LaGravenese's script had a scene in Grand Central Station where commuters are struck by the beauty of a street performer's song. Gilliam revised it to make it more cinematic and the result is a breathtakingly lovely moment when the passengers, including jaded New Yorkers, Hassidic Jews, and a flock of nuns in traditional wimples do a graceful waltz throughout the station as Parry and Lydia walk through, seemingly unaware. Perhaps it is an outward manifestation of the magic between them or perhaps we are seeing through Parry's unreliable vision. Former Washington Post movie critic Desson Thomson calls it the film's "crowning moment," saying

> *As Williams waits for Plummer to pass, the station (in his reverie) becomes an ornate ballroom. The commuters suddenly dance with each other in a delirious waltz. Before Williams can claim Plummer as a partner, however, a bell goes off. The dancers become commuters and the working world rushes back in. In this, Gilliam is in his element -- leaping effortlessly from one world to another.*

More from Terry Gilliam:

"Brazil"

"Time Bandits"

"Twelve Monkeys"

"Fear and Loathing in Las Vegas"

§ § §

42

FRIENDLY PERSUASION
(1956)

Everyone Draws the Line Somewhere

The movie: Based on the novel by Jessamyn West, this is the story of the Birdwells, a loving Quaker family in the midst of the Civil War, trying to reconcile their commitment to non-violence with their responsibility to their community.

A Union soldier comes to the Quaker prayer meeting to ask the men to join the army. They tell him that they cannot engage in violence under any circumstances. "We are opposed to slavery, but do not think it right to kill one man to free another." Even when the soldier points out that this means others will be dying to protect their lives and property, they insist that they cannot participate in killing.

Eliza Birdwell (Dorothy McGuire), a devout woman, is the moral center of the family. Her husband Jess (Gary Cooper) is a thoughtful and highly principled man, but not as strict as Eliza. Their children are Joshua (Anthony Perkins), a sensitive young man who opposes violence but feels that he must join the soldiers; Mattie (Phyllis Love), who falls in love with a non-Quaker Union soldier; and Young Jess, a boy who is fascinated with the talk of war and battles. Each member of the family finds his or her beliefs tested, and each ultimately responds with humility and integrity. This is a rare movie in which characters pray for guidance, and a rare movie that shows how families can find a way to live together and support each other even when they disagree.

Joshua finds that he is morally obligated to join the fight, though he weeps when he kills a Confederate soldier. Jess, takes the gun from a sniper who shot his friend but will not harm him. He tells the gunman, "Go on, get! I'll not harm thee." As the war approaches their doorstep, Jess and Eliza refuse to run away from their farm as others are doing.

This is an exceptional depiction of a loving family, particularly for the way that Jess and Eliza work together on resolving their conflicts. They listen to each other with enormous respect and deep affection. Jess does his best to go along with Eliza's stricter views on observance, because in his heart he believes she is right. Nevertheless, he cannot keep himself from trying to have his horse outrun his friend's as they go to church on Sunday. And he cannot give up music. Cooper's face when he sees an organ is a marvel of irrepressible pleasure. He decides to buy it, knowing that Eliza will object. She says that she forbids it, to which he replies mildly, "When thee asks or suggests, I am like putty in thy hands, but when thee forbids, thee is barking up the wrong tree." She will not stay in the house with the musical instrument, so she decides to sleep in the barn. Jess does not object -- but he goes out there to spend the night with her, and they reconcile and find

a way to compromise.

All of this provides a counterpoint to more serious questions of faith and conscience, beautifully presented through characters who make the story absorbing, but with an underlying structure that shows us a range of responses.

The moment: The Confederates ride into the farm, and in keeping with her faith, Eliza welcomes them and gives them all her food, even knowing that they may have been shooting at her son, may even have killed him. But when one of the soldiers goes after her beloved pet goose, she whacks him with the broom, amusing her children and leaving herself disconcerted and embarrassed. Even she discovers she has her limits in this warm-hearted but forthright story.

Other movie Quakers:

"High Noon"

"Cheyenne Autumn"

"The Angel and the Badman"

§ § §

43

Galaxy Quest
(1999)

Hitting the Blue Button

The movie: "Star Trek" was a failed television series of the late 1960's that became a phenomenon. The original series with Kirk and Spock was kept on the air for a third season only because of a frantic letter-writing campaign. Even then, Trek fans were devoted. But they could not keep it on past the third season. Through the 1970's it became even more popular in syndication and since then it has been rebooted five times on television and in eleven feature films -- so far.

Trek fans are so passionate that at least three documentaries have been made about the fans and the show: the irresistible "Trekkies" (with the all-Trek dental office, "Hamlet" in Klingon, and a self-dubbed "Spiner Femme," a woman fan with notebooks filled with pictures of Data performer Brent Spiner), "Trekkies 2" (the international fans) and "The Captains," with original series' James Tiberius Kirk (William Shatner) interviewing his successor captains and visiting a Star Trek convention. These gatherings are legendary for the dedicated fervor of the fans and of course they gather at other events as well.

Once at Comic-Con in San Diego I overheard a bunch of Trekkers (their preferred term) asking, "What time is the Klingon wedding?" Klingon is one of the most extensive and widely used conlangs (constructed languages). It was developed by Mark Okrand, a specialist in Native American languages (he also created the language for the residents of Atlantis in the Disney film by that name). Works like *The Epic of Gilgamesh* and *Much Ado About Nothing* have been translated into Klingon.

It is easy to make fun of all of this. It is not easy to create a combination tribute and spoof, but that is what David Howard did with "Galaxy Quest," one of the funniest movies of the 1990's. What makes it so funny is that it comes from a very deep place of love for the show and its fans.

"Galaxy Quest" stars Tim Allen, Sigourney Weaver, Tony Shaloub, and Alan Rickman as actors who once starred on a "Star Trek"-like series and now spend their days living off their former fame and their loyal fans. They discover that those fans include some real-life aliens who believe the shows they saw were historical documents and who have created a real-life spaceship that replicates the one on the show.

They show up to ask the actors they think are in reality the characters they played to join them in fighting a nasty spiky-scaly bad guy with the obligatory English accent. The actors have to resolve their own issues and learn some lessons before they can live up to the characters they once created.

The better you know "Star Trek" and other space series, the more you will appreciate this brilliantly constructed film. The nerdy fan (a first appearance by Justin Long), the slumming classically trained British actor (Rickman), the actress whose character's only job on the show was to repeat everything the computer said (Weaver), the actor who appeared on only one episode and fears he is a glorified extra but hopes he's the "plucky comic relief" -- even the aliens are expertly drawn and sublimely acted. The sci-fi elements are solid, the special effects are excellent, and the plot works on every level.

The moment: The captain (Allen) and communications officer (Weaver) are sent on a typical sci-fi mission. Some sort of automatic, self-destruct, blow-up-the-ship program has been activated and they have to find the reset button to stop it. This is what movie types call a "tick-tock." Time is counting down and the ship's computer helpfully keeps us up to speed by telling us that we are 45 seconds from being blown to smithereens, then 44.... Many close calls occur on the way there (all both scary and funny) as the nerdy fans back on earth use their mastery of the series' minutiae to guide them through the inner labyrinth of the ship's interior.

Just in time, the actors make it, and only 12 seconds from blow-up, the faux captain hits the blue button. Relief is quickly displaced by horror as the time clock continues to count down. Then they realize why it is still going. The ship they are on has been meticulously created to be identical to the spaceship on the show in every detail. And on the show, the crisis cannot be averted until it counts down to 1. Of course.

More comic sci-fi:

"Spaceballs"

"The Hitchhiker's Guide to the Galaxy"

"Mars Attacks!"

§ § §

44

The General
(1926)

Buster Keaton Gets Some Help

The movie: Buster Keaton's parents were vaudevillians who owned a travelling show with magician Harry Houdini. Keaton often said that he got the name "Buster" when Houdini, seeing him fall down the stairs as a small child, landing without crying or getting hurt, said, "What a buster!" Keaton, one of the biggest stars of the early years of cinema, was known for his stoic expression, often used for comic effect, and was referred to as "The Great Stone Face."

Keaton was not only a star, but a writer and director. Like most of the stars of the early rough and tumble years of cinema, he also did his own stunts, and he was a master of timing and precision. In "Steamboat Bill, Jr." he stood as the entire two-ton fascade of a two-story house fell down, missing him by inches because Keaton the director was careful to make sure that Keaton the performer was standing underneath an open window. For the same movie, he brought in six wind machines that made it possible for him to lean in at a 45-degree angle as buildings were being blown down all around him. Jackie Chan always says that Keaton is his most important inspiration, and when you watch Keaton you can see how Chan was influenced by Keaton's impeccable grace and timing.

"The General" is based on a real incident of the Civil War. Keaton plays Southerner Johnny Gray, who has two great loves. One is the beautiful Annabelle (Marion Mack).

The other is the train, known as "The General." When war breaks out, he tries to enlist but is rejected because he is too valuable to the Confederacy as an engineer. Annabelle does not understand and says she will not speak to him until he is a soldier like her father and brother.

The Union Army captures the General, with Annabelle on it. Johnny sets off to get both of them back. The two chases that ensue, one to get the train back and the second to warn the Confederates of an upcoming Union raid, are still some of the most thrilling ever captured on screen, and without so much as a pixel of CGI. Everything you see actually happened in front of the camera and it is a timeless masterpiece of cinematic storytelling as well as an adrenaline rush of the first order. This is a gorgeous film that really benefits from being seen in a theater.

The moment: About two-thirds of the way through the movie, Annabelle decides to help Johnny keep the train running by stoking the fire. In her refined way, as he is shoveling as much wood into the flames as he can, she rejects one piece because it has a hole in it, tossing precious fuel away, and daintily tosses a more suitable stick into the furnace. He watches her in disbelief, then solicitously hands her a tiny splinter to see if it suits her sensibilities. She helpfully tosses it into the fire. He grabs her, quickly (teasingly) chokes her, and then hugs her - about the most eloquent ten seconds in movie history about the frustrations and joys of relationships.

More Buster Keaton:

"Steamboat Bill, Jr."

"Sherlock Jr."

"The Cameraman"

"The Navigator"

45

GIANT
(1956)

Jett Rink Strikes Oil

The movie: "Giant" is as sprawling as the Texas it depicts, a two-generation, three hour and seventeen minute saga based on the epic book by Edna Ferber. The image of Reata, the huge, ornate home outlined against the stark flatness of the bleak Texas landscape, is one of the icons of American film.

Jordan "Bick" Benedict (Rock Hudson) is a Texas rancher who goes to Maryland to buy a horse named War Winds. He meets Leslie Lynnton (Elizabeth Taylor), they get married, and they arrive at Reata. Bick's sister, Luz (Mercedes McCambridge), who owns the ranch, is not happy about the marriage and is unfriendly to Leslie.

Luz insists on digging her spurs into War Winds, who bucks and throws her off. She is killed, leaving Reata to Bick except for a small portion she leaves to ranch worker Jett Rink (James Dean). Bick tries to buy it back, but Jett is obstinate and refuses, partly to annoy Bick and partly because he loves Leslie.

The moment: One of the themes of the film is the impact of the oil industry on the ranch-based communities of Texas. This is evocatively demonstrated in a scene that has Bick, Leslie, and their friends and family enjoying a gathering on the porch. Everyone is wearing pale colors, with Bick and Leslie in white and cream. Jett's filthy black rattletrap of a truck approaches, cutting across the lawn.

He gets out, covered with sticky, black oil. He has hit a gusher on his small property and he wants them to know it, and he wants them to know that it changes everything. He approaches the house, sinuous as a mountain lion, drunk with the thrill of money and power, and embodying danger. Emboldened by what he sees as his new equivalence with his former employer, he says,

> *It's here, and there ain't a dang thing you gonna do about it! My well came in big, so big, Bick and there's more down there and there's bigger wells. I'm rich, Bick. I'm a rich 'un. I'm a rich boy. Me, I'm gonna have more money than you ever thought you could have, you and all the rest of you stinkin' sons of...Benedicts!*

Leslie tries to calm him down, but he is too far gone. He deliberately puts his oil-covered hand on the pristine white column, leans on it, and speaks insolently to her, telling her she is pretty enough to eat. Bick punches him, and Jett punches back, then drives off. Bick's uncle says, "You shoulda shot that fellow a long time ago. Now he's too rich to kill."

Director George Stevens makes this scene riveting on two levels. One is the explosive impact of Jett himself on the two Benedicts. The mesmerizing Dean, in his last role before he was killed at age 24 in a car accident, has such incendiary screen chemistry that he effortlessly holds his own with the nine-inches-taller Hudson and the no-slouch-in-the-screen-chemistry Taylor. The way he places his filthy hand on the spotless column is electrifying.

The other level is his symbolic representation of the wildcat, instantly super-rich oil industry on the staid, slow, world of ranching, a world that thought of itself as more gentlemanly and civilized. Bick refuses at first to allow drilling on his land, just as (exploring another of the movie's themes) he refuses at first to reconsider his racist prejudices.

One other point worth mentioning -- the characters age decades over the course of the film. There is something eerie and disturbing about Dean's appearing on screen as a middle-aged man because it reminds us that we never got to see him age in real life.

More from James Dean:

"East of Eden"

"Rebel Without a Cause"

§ § §

46

The Godfather, Part 2
(1974)

Back to the Beginning

The movie: The two "Godfather" movies are a masterpiece in every category, with an epic sweep and an operatic rise and fall story. Director Francis Ford Coppola makes every detail of setting, design, lighting, dialog, acting, and music fascinatingly specific to a world of treachery where making a wrong decision or backing the wrong person can be fatal. Each of these elements is worth examining in depth, but I am only going to focus on one element of the second film to illustrate non-linear storytelling.

Many films play with non-linear narrative, perhaps most notably "Citizen Kane," which begins with a newsreel that summarizes the title character's life and then goes back and forth as a present-day reporter interviews people who knew Kane. A mosaic portrait emerges, but the film leaves the final answer and the further questions it raises to us. "Betrayal" would have been a conventional story of an affair and its aftermath if it were told from beginning to end. But Harold Pinter's play and the movie version give us the end first, with nine scenes that go back in time to the careless and impulsive decision, which we now see in the context of its consequences over seven years. "The Hangover" would have been a forgettable movie about a wild night if not for its clever structure that has the characters and the audience piecing together what happened the next day. And one of the best episodes of the "Seinfeld" television series was also called "The Betrayal," in tribute to Pinter. It told the story of a trip to India for a wedding in reverse chronology. As in "The Hangover," we learn in hilarious fashion what led to the disarray we witness at the beginning, which is really the end.

When the two "Godfather" movies were shown on network television in 1977, Coppola recut them and added some previously deleted scenes for a miniseries he called "The Godfather: A Novel for Television." While the additional scenes were of interest, more for revelation of character than for plot or thematic reasons, the biggest difference was the re-alignment of the original scenes to follow the story chronologically from early 20th century Sicily to Las Vegas, Nevada in 1959. It works better in its original form.

The theatrical release of the first "Godfather" follows Michael Corleone (Al Pacino), the son of crime boss Vito Corleone (Marlon Brando) from his idealistic hope of staying out of the family business ("That's my father, Kay, not me," he tells the woman he hopes to marry, still wearing the uniform of his military service during WWII) through a series of choices that take him deeper and deeper into the darkness of crime and isolation from his humanity. But the second movie goes back and forth in time. It is both sequel and prequel for the first one. We see Michael continuing to become more spiritually corrupted by ambition, revenge, and suspicion. And we see Vito as a young man (played by Robert De Niro) from his Sicilian childhood, where his family is killed by a local Mafia don, through his arrival in the United States, his marriage, his first involvement in crime, his murder of a local small-time don and his return to Sicily to kill the man who killed his family.

Each development in Vito's story illuminates Michael's. Each development in Michael's story shows us how Vito's choices directed Michael's. And then, Coppola makes one more shift in time for an ending that brings the two stories together.

The moment: In the next-to-last scene, set in 1941, we go 18 years back for Michael and 16 years forward for Vito. It is Vito's birthday and his children are waiting for him to come home and celebrate. The smallest details have enormous import for us because we know what they will mean. Sonny (James Caan), whose brutal murder we saw early in the first film, is there, young and hotheaded. He has brought a friend to meet his sister, Vito's only daughter Connie. It is Carlo, whose wedding to Connie will begin the first movie and whose murder will show us how far Michael will go and how far he has fallen. Sonny says anyone who fights "for strangers" is a sap. Michael quietly says it is fighting for his country, and he tells Sonny he has enlisted. Sonny is furious. When their other brother, Fredo (John Cazale) tries to shake Michael's hand, Sonny slaps it away. Tom Hagan (Robert Duvall) tells Michael that he and Vito had plans for him. Michael says he had his own plans. We hear Vito arriving in the next room and everyone else runs out to greet him, but Michael stays behind, and then we are back in the movie's present day again, 1959, Michael sitting alone, perhaps wondering whose plans got him where he is.

More experiments with non-linear story-telling:

"Pulp Fiction"

"Stardust Memories"

"Out of Sight"

"The Killing"

"Memento"

47

GOLD DIGGERS OF 1933
(1933)

Ere-Way In-Way the Oney-May

The movie: Lady Gaga's trippiest numbers hark back to the delirious madness of the musical performances choreographed by Busby Berkeley. You want to see endless rows of girls waving enormous bananas? A waterfall of girls? Girls waving their legs to make kaleidoscopic patterns? Or lining up to make a giant violin, with a row of girls playing the part of the bow? Berkeley will show you!

Berkeley understood that movies could transform the way we watch dancers. Instead of putting a stationary camera down in what would be the sixth row center of the theater and letting us get the view of a good seat in a live theater, he made the camera part of the choreography, zooming through dozens of lovely legs and panning up or shooting down from the ceiling to give us views no one had ever seen before.

Mervyn LeRoy directed "Gold Diggers of 1933" and its saucy, pre-Hays Code script about chorus girls who marry well is only fair but it has a pleasantly insouciant tone. It is the story of four aspiring actresses, one sweet (Ruby Keeler), one sassy (Aline MacMahon), one passionate (Joan Blondell), and one glamorous (Ginger Rogers), who try to put on a show despite hard times with the help of their talented singer-songwriter neighbor (Dick Powell). He will not tell them where he got the money they need.

What is memorable is the musical numbers created by Busby Berkeley that stand out, even with some sub-par songs from the usually reliable Harry Warren and Al Dubin. "Pettin' in the Park" is notable only because its lyrics are rather racy compared to those that would be permitted a year later following enforcement of the already-adopted the Hays Code that would keep films squeaky clean for more than three decades. "Shadow Waltz" is where we get a sense of the scope of Berkeley's vision with glow-in-the-dark violins and stunning effects from overhead and sideways shots, swirling three-tiered hoop skirts requiring two thousand yards of China silk, and a reflecting pool.

But "Remember My Forgotten Man" is a searing and surprisingly powerful song, the great anthem of the Depression era. It is performed by Joan Blondell and an uncredited Etta Moten, who that year became the first black performer to appear at the White House. She would later create the role of Bess in George Gershwin's "Porgy and Bess" on Broadway. Blondell's singing voice in this number is dubbed by the great Marian Anderson. And you can get a glimpse of Berkeley himself as the call boy who yells, "Everybody on stage for the 'Forgotten Man' number!"

The moment: In the movie's joyously surreal opening musical number, Ginger Rogers, bedecked in golden coins, and surrounded by chorus girls, sings "We're in the Money" in the middle of the Depression. In Pig Latin. And the chorus girls do a proto-version of The Wave with big fake coins.

More from Busby Berkeley:

"Footlight Parade"

"Babes on Broadway"

"The Gang's All Here"

48

Harper
(1966)

The Hero Starts His Day

The movie: One of the most difficult challenges for filmmakers is introducing us to the hero of the story. They have about five minutes to get us to fall in love - or at least in fascination - with the lead figure, to make us eager to spend the next two hours rooting for him or her. Even if it is an anti-hero, there has to be something immediate that grabs us. Most of the movie will be about presenting the lead character with a dilemma and seeing how he or she resolves it. But if we do not care about the character, it does not matter how interesting the dilemma is, how impressive the stunts and special effects are, how beautiful the actors, or how outrageously funny the situation.

One of the greatest movie opens of all time is the sensational action sequence at the beginning of "Raiders of the Lost Ark." As Indiana Jones (Harrison Ford) reaches and takes the idol and escapes all of the booby-traps and treachery to get it out of the cave, only to have to hand it over to his arch-rival, we learn that he is brave, smart, quick-thinking, and capable. He gets our sympathy because Dr. Belloq (Paul Freeman) takes something through force that Indy gained through courage and skill. We do not fall in love with Indy, though, until the next scene, when, rescued by a friend in a plane, we at last get to see him rattled. "I hate snakes!" Now he is human and vulnerable, and self-aware, and we will be on his side for this movie and three sequels.

Another sublime introduction to the lead characters is the Beatles' first film, "A Hard Day's Night." Director Richard Lester and often unfairly overlooked screenwriter Alun Owen were so good that many people think the film is a documentary. But it was carefully and precisely scripted and the opening sequence is brilliantly designed to delight the viewers who were already Beatles fans but also to engage those who were skeptical or even hostile to the group when many were still appalled by their long hair and different sound. To make it even more difficult, they had to introduce us to four different characters at once. As the fans chase after the group, within the space of one song on the soundtrack, we meet the Beatles. And instead of any awe or resentment we might feel for their success, they gain our instant sympathy by being portrayed as fun-loving but sincere guys who are trying to stay on top of the madness around them.

William Goldman had already written the screenplay for "Harper," based on a detective novel by Ross Macdonald, and the first cut of the movie had been filmed and sent to the studio when Goldman was asked to write something to go under the opening credits. It was a last-minute addition that is still one of the best meet-the-hero moments on screen and he has said it is one of the most frequently mentioned to him by fans.

The moment: Harper (Paul Newman) wakes up in a small, cluttered apartment. He wants coffee. There is none left. So, he reaches into the garbage can, pulls out the grounds from the day before, and puts it into the coffee maker, adds hot water, takes a sip, and grimly smiles. He is not very good at providing for himself, but he is very good at solving problems and making do. This economical and very cinematic introduction tells us what most screenwriters would need five pages of script to convey.

More great meet-the-hero moments:

"Citizen Kane"

"Bridget Jones' Diary"

"In the Heat of the Night"

"Patton"

"Oliver!"

"Fargo"

§ § §

49

HIGH TIME
(1960)

Time Passes

The movie: "High Time" is an entertaining trifle that is enjoyable but not especially memorable. It is a lesser work from director Blake Edwards ("Breakfast at Tiffany's," "The Days of Wine and Roses," "The Pink Panther") and star Bing Crosby, just a light comedy about a successful middle-aged businessman who decides to get the college experience he never had.

He wants more than the classes and teachers. He wants the whole college experience, living in the dorm, silly freshman fraternity hazing, and even romance (with a pretty French professor). Best remembered now for introducing the lovely song, "The Second Time Around," or for inspiring the far coarser Rodney Dangerfield vehicle "Back to School," I'm including it here because it is a good example of one of the trickiest challenges in movie story-telling, denoting the passage of time.

Just as the first filmgoers jumped back when they saw an onrushing train on the big screen, they were confused about how to know whether and how much time had passed in the story. Today we are used to the conventions that movies use to signify the passage of time, but the cinematic vocabulary of temporal indicators had to be developed and some work better than others. The man who was the real pioneer in conveying a sense of time on screen was the Serbian-American film director, editor, cinematographer, and scholar Slavko

Vorkapich. If you have ever seen calendar pages flying off or a clock's hands sped up to let you know how much time had passed, you have seen a Vorkapich effect.

In films like "David Copperfield" and "Mr. Smith Goes to Washington," he used kinetic editing, lap dissolves (one shot fades into the next), tracking shots (the camera movies along a track), creative graphics and optical effects to give the audience a sense of what happened over the period of time that elapsed. The montages we see when athletes are training or couples are falling in love or characters are traveling or becoming more or less successful or big projects are being completed are all based on Vorkapich's techniques.

Still, some films get it wrong. I will not embarrass the filmmakers by giving the name of a low-budget indie I once saw that kept telling us months had passed but showed the main character wearing the same parka, walking past the same snowy landscape. Clearly, while the script went over many months, the shooting schedule covered only a couple of weeks. Even though the script said winter was over, they did not have the budget to make it look like there were leaves on the trees or the sense to have the characters wear spring clothes.

I like creative, highly cinematic temporal indicators, and wish more filmmakers would feel comfortable using them. In one of the most conventional of movies, "Notting Hill," all of a sudden there is a scene of Hugh Grant walking through an open market, his jacket over his shoulder, as "Ain't No Sunshine" plays on the soundtrack. He passes a pregnant woman and keeps walking. It begins to rain and umbrellas go up everywhere. He puts on his jacket, but it is not until it starts snowing that we are certain we have (briefly) left the literal world for an impressionistic depiction of months going by. He keeps walking and then the sun is out, spring flowers are all over the market, and woman who was pregnant at the beginning is holding a baby who is a couple of months old. We know not just that time has passed, but that Grant's character has felt isolated all that time. My friend, movie critic Mark Jenkins, reminds me of the segue from bone to monolith in "2001: A Space Odyssey" and the match to the desert in "Lawrence of Arabia" as vivid expressions of the passage of time.

In the George Pal version of "The Time Machine" we see time pass through the changes in a store window. And in the beginning of the great Michael Powell/Emeric Pressburger film, "The Red Shoes," there is a nice contrast between the thundering rush and high spirits of the students racing into the theater to grab the best of the cheap seats and the crawl across the bottom of the screen "Forty-five minutes later," without any cuts or dissolves, showing them patiently waiting as they eat their sandwiches. Perhaps the all-time best indicator of the passage of time and its consequences is in the series of breakfasts showing Charles Foster Kane and his wife literally further apart in "Citizen Kane," the last one showing her reading the rival newspaper.

The moment: Because it covers four years of college, "High Time" lends itself well to what in television are called "interstitials," little between-scene bookends. As the freshmen sit in their first orientation, a close-up of Crosby and his co-stars (including pop star Fabian and Richard Beymer just before he would appear as Tony in "West Side Story") freezes to a still picture. Then group of brightly clad underclassmen come out with paintbrushes, cover it with bright blue, and then paint the word "freshman" over it. Later, students push snow away from the frame to show that winter has arrived. Accompanied by Henry Mancini's bright theme music, these small interjections of time indicators are frankly artificial, with impossible angles that separate them from the "realistic" world of the film, and yet they only add to its brightness and sense of fun.

More college comedies:
- "Animal House"
- "Monkey Business"
- "PCU"
- "Good News"

§ § §

50

Hobson's Choice (1954)

The Morning After the Wedding Night

The movie: Director David Lean is most often remembered for sweeping epics ("Lawrence of Arabia," "Doctor Zhivago") and superb adaptations of Charles Dickens ("Great Expectations," "Oliver Twist"). But he also made a charming domestic romantic comedy with "Hobson's Choice," set in the late 19th century. It is the story of a bombastic father of three young women who work for him in his shoe store..

"Hobson's choice" is an expression meaning no real choice at all, a "take it or leave it" proposition. In this story, it refers to the way Henry Horatio Hobson (Charles Laughton) runs his family and his store. His two younger daughters have boyfriends but he refuses to let them get married because he is too cheap to pay a dowry and he wants them to keep working in the store and taking care of him.

The oldest daughter, Maggie (Brenda De Banzie) does not have a boyfriend, but she has an eye on the shop's very talented cobbler, Will Mossop (John Mills). He is uneducated, shy, and lower class, but she sees potential in him and orders him he must marry her. He is overwhelmed and reluctant at first, but Hobson's efforts to stop them gives him resolve and soon he is inspired by Maggie's vision of a much greater sense of possibilities.

In the New York Times, critic Bosley Crowther called Laughton's performance "the windy and bibulous curmudgeon right down to the ground. From his somewhat voluminous entrance on the crest of a characteristic belch, he is the utter personification of pompous egoism and stinginess. A pinchfist of mammoth proportions and a fat-head of bloated conceits, he is wicked and funny and pitiful, separately and on the whole." But more than half a century later, Laughton's drunken antics do not hold up as well as the Will/Maggie story.

Even though it can never have the power to shock a modern audience long accustomed to marriages across class (and many other) lines, their love story is very affecting. Maggie is brusque and inconsiderate and at first their relationship seems exploitive. She directs him like a drill sergeant, ordering him to quit his job, dump his girlfriend, and marry her.

The day they get married, they invite her two sisters and their boyfriends to celebrate with them in their tiny little shop/apartment. Maggie traps her father into attending and then into providing dowries for her sisters.

Everyone leaves and Maggie gives Will his regular nightly lesson in writing. His assignment: copying over the sentence, "There is always room at the top." Then she gets ready for bed and in a scene of exquisitely played pantomime we see

him slowly remove his jacket, his false shirt front and cuffs, and get into his nightshirt, looking terrified. "I'm ready," she calls out, and he swallows hard and goes into the bedroom.

The moment: The next morning, she is all bustle getting breakfast and opening the shop. He comes out of the bedroom in his work clothes and just gazes at her, then stops her and gives her a tender kiss. In that moment, we see that what passed between them the night before has re-aligned the relationship so that they are truly equals. Before the wedding, she told him that the minister would ask if he loved her. If he could not answer "yes" truthfully she told him not to answer at all. He told her it would be a truthful "yes."

In the brief morning moment before their first customer arrives to buy bootlaces for a penny, we see that it has become a genuine love match for them both, and that each sees more in the other than anyone has before, even themselves. That 30 seconds is one of the sweetest depictions of love ever filmed.

More Charles Laughton:

"Witness for the Prosecution"

"Advise and Consent"

"The Canterville Ghost"

"Night of the Hunter" (director)

§ § §

51

Holiday
(1938)

Cary Grant Flips

The movie: "The Philadelphia Story" is one of the most-beloved films of all time, 44 on the American Film Institute's list of the greatest films of all time and 15 on their list of top comedies. "Holiday" has the same playwright, screenwriter, director, and stars, and deserves to be better remembered.

After a whirlwind romance at a ski resort, Johnny Case (Cary Grant) sees that the address given him by his new fiancée, Julia Seton (Doris Nolan) is a mansion and he assumes she must be on the staff. But she is the daughter of the wealthy and distinguished family that occupies the house. He is surprised and amused, and enjoys meeting Julia's sister Linda (Katherine Hepburn) and brother Ned (Lew Ayres). They promise to help him win over their father, who is likely to object to the engagement, because Johnny is not from an upper-class wealthy family.

Johnny is a poor boy who has worked hard and done very well. Julia likes him because she sees a similarity to her grandfather, who made a fortune. She wants him to do the same, and tells him, "There's nothing more exciting than making money." But Johnny, who has just taken the first vacation of his life, only wants to make enough so that he can take a "holiday," to "find out why I've been working." As the movie begins, he is about to achieve that goal.

Linda thinks this is a great idea. She is something of an outsider in the family, forsaking the huge formal rooms of the mansion for one cozy room upstairs, which she calls "the only home I've got." She tries to persuade Julia and their father that Johnny is right.

One weakness in the film is the impossibility of believing that even for a moment Johnny could have thought he was in love with Julia. We know long before he does that he'll end up with Linda but it unfolds nicely and there are some lovely moments including two exceptionally appealing characters in Johnny's friends the Potters, played by Jean Dixon and Edward Everett Horton. Their kindness, generosity, and wisdom contrast with the superficial values of the Seton family in some sharp exchanges. Lew Ayres is heartbreaking as the brother who wishes he could have the courage to defy the family but instead just drinks. "I'll be back for you," Linda tells him. "I'll be…here," he replies.

The moment: Grant got his start as an acrobat and that training and skill is evident in his unparalleled timing and grace as an actor. Critic Richard Shickel called him "the acrobat of the living room." "Holiday" is a very rare opportunity to get a glimpse of his gymnastic skill as he and Katherine Hepburn do a couple of tricks up in her special room.

More Cary Grant:

"The Philadelphia Story"

"Charade"

"My Favorite Wife"

"His Girl Friday

§ § §

52

HOMICIDAL
(1961)

Fright Break

The movie: Filmmaker William Castle was closer to P.T. Barnum than to Stephen Spielberg. He will not be remembered for his stories, characters, dialog, or cinematic storytelling but his showmanship and his wild stunts are still legendary. His low-budget thriller films were unapologetically cheesy and derivative, usually made with justifiably unknown performers. But his marketing efforts were unparalleled for cheeky, wild imagination and that made the experience of seeing his films silly, over-the-top fun.

Castle was involved with some memorable films, including "The Lady from Shanghai," where he was an assistant to Orson Welles, and particularly "Rosemary's Baby," where he was a producer and even appeared on screen as the man with gray hair outside the phone booth while Mia Farrow was trying to call her doctor. But far better than any of the films Castle directed is "Matinee," an affectionate movie inspired by his antics, directed by Joe Dante, with John Goodman in the lead role. There's also an excellent documentary called "Spine Tingler!: The William Castle Story."

In 1958, Castle released "Macabre," written by frequent collaborator Robb White (the father of NPR commentator and writer Bailey White). The only thing memorable about the film, a grisly story of a doctor who has five hours to rescue his daughter, who was buried alive, was the advertising gimmick: Castle took out a thousand-dollar life insurance policy certified by Lloyd's of London to cover anyone who died of shock while viewing the film and audience members were presented with a certificate as they entered the theater.

"The Tingler," again written by White, had Vincent Price as a doctor with a theory that there is a creature called "the tingler" inside all of us that creates the sensation of fear, and can only be suppressed by screaming. He uses LSD (its first on-screen depiction) to induce fear in a mute woman who cannot scream. Castle created a gimmick called "Percepto." (Castle loved to add the letter "O" to a word to name his innovations.) Hidden buzzers would vibrate seats in the theater when the tingler (a larger version of the real-life creature called the velvet worm) appeared on screen. He also paid shills to sit in the theater and shriek, which might have dis-

tracted real audience members from noticing the wires moving the fake-looking tingler.

For "The House on Haunted Hill," again written by White, he invented "Emergo," a real-life inflatable glow-in-the-dark skeleton swooped out from the screen at the movie's climax. "13 Ghosts" had special "Illusion-O" viewers for the audience with red and blue cellophane panels. If they wanted to see the ghosts on screen, they could look through the red side. But if the ghosts were too scary, they could watch through the blue side. For "I Saw What You Did," he had seat-belts installed on seats in the theater so the audience members would not be jolted from their seats in terror. Ticket-buyers for "Mr. Sardonicus" were given cards with glow-in-the-dark green thumbs to hold up or down for a "punishment poll" to determine whether the title character would be cured or die at the end of the film. Castle himself appeared onscreen to explain the process, but there is no evidence to suggest that Mr. Sardonicus was ever given a happy ending.

But his best gimmick of all was in "Homicidal." The heir to a family fortune returns home after a long absence as he is about to turn 21. Accompanying him are his former nurse, now an invalid after a stroke, mute and confined to a wheelchair, and a mysterious blond.

The moment: As often happens in thrillers, there comes a point near the climax when a character is warned not to go into a dark, menacing house. Of course, she goes anyway, but before she does, the movie gives us a "fright break." A stopwatch on screen counts down 45 seconds to give those who are too terrified to find out what is inside that house to leave and get their money back. According to director John Waters, a Castle fan, when people actually took advantage of this offer,

> William Castle simply went nuts. He came up with "Coward's Corner," a yellow cardboard booth, manned

by a bewildered theater employee in the lobby. When the Fright Break was announced, and you found that you couldn't take it any more, you had to leave your seat and, in front of the entire audience, follow yellow footsteps up the aisle, bathed in a yellow light. Before you reached Coward's Corner, you crossed yellow lines with the stenciled message: "Cowards Keep Walking." You passed a nurse (in a yellow uniform?...I wonder), who would offer a blood-pressure test. All the while a recording was blaring, "Watch the chicken! Watch him shiver in Coward's Corner!" As the audience howled, you had to go through one final indignity -- at Coward's Corner you were forced to sign a yellow card stating, "I am a bona fide coward." Very, very few were masochistic enough to endure this. The one percent refund dribbled away to a zero percent, and I'm sure that in many cities a plant had to be paid to go through this torture.

I hope there were no more takers. The surprise in the house is pretty wild!

More from William Castle:

"13 Ghosts"

"The Tingler"

"I Saw What You Did"

"Let's Kill Uncle"

§ § §

53

Hoop Dreams (1994)

Not the Graduation You Expect

The movie: "People always say to me, 'When you get to the NBA, don't forget about me.' Well, I should've said back, 'If I don't make it to the NBA, don't you forget about me.'"

This heart-wrenchingly poignant quote comes at the end of the groundbreaking documentary that Roger Ebert called the greatest film of the 1990's, "Hoop Dreams."

Over four years, a dedicated documentary team led by Steve James, Frederick Marx, and Peter Gilbert, followed the lives of two promising inner city high school basketball players and their families. Arthur Agee and William Gates were initially given athletic scholarships to a prestigious private school, alma mater of NBA star Isiah Thomas, but then Agee's scholarship is cut off when his skills (and his height) do not meet the coach's expectations.

The boys and their families dream of using their basketball skills to get to college, and then to the NBA. Where they are, even that .00005 percent chance seems a better bet than any of their other alternatives for making it out of the inner city.

This extraordinary film is one of the most perceptive and involving portraits of America ever made. Its portrayal of these families and its messages about race, class, family, and American notions of success are unforgettable. There is heartbreak and triumph on and off the basketball court. We also see the way that the filmmakers themselves got caught up in the story. In one scene, when a family's power is turned off because they did not pay the electricity bill, it is the filmmakers who chip in to get the lights back on. It may be contrary to every rule of journalism and documentary filmmaking, but anything else would be contrary to every principle of ethics and humanity.

It is filled with scenes of extraordinary power and insight as the filmmakers keep the camera running and let the story unfold. In one, Agee's family is told that not only is his scholarship being cut off but the family will be expected to reimburse the school for some of the money he received. In another, Agee's father comes to watch him shoot hoops on a playground, and then wanders off. We see him buying drugs in the background while the camera focuses on Agee's face as he struggles to maintain his composure.

The moment: The scene that says the most, though, is not about the boys and it is not about basketball. Arthur Agee's mother Sheila graduates from a program that certifies her as a nurse's assistant. It is a moment of great triumph for her, and one of the few purely joyous scenes in the film. Actor/filmmaker Nelson Carvjal wrote:

> *Because this scene doesn't come near the end of "Hoop Dreams" we don't see Sheila's graduation as a conclusive victory but rather as a tragic foil to the bigger picture of the culture's obsession with the mostly elusive basketball dream. Notice the closing shot of Sheila's graduation: the camera is almost outside of the room, showing rows upon empty rows of vacant seats.*

The contrast between the importance of this victory to Sheila and the limited impact it will have on her family's quality of life, and the even greater contrast between the tiny group attending the graduation and the packed audience at the basketball game that follows is searing.

More sports documentaries that transcend the genre:
- "Heart of the Game"
- "When We Were Kings"
- "Once in a Lifetime"
- "Undefeated"
- "Murderball"
- "Dogtown and Z-Boys"
- "The Life and Times of Hank Greenberg"

§ § §

54

Houseboat (1958)

A Quick Fix

The movie: "Houseboat" was popular when it was released and was even nominated for two Oscars, for best song and best screenplay. It is by no means a classic and is not often remembered but it is a very worthwhile family film with romance, comedy, and heart, and gorgeous stars with great chemistry: Cary Grant and Sophia Loren. Highlights include not just the nominated song ("Almost in Your Arms") but the bouncy "Bing Bang Boom" and the "Who Sir, Me Sir" game Grant's character teaches his children. It is a rare film where Grant plays a father, and there is a very touching scene where he talks to his son (Paul Peterson of "The Donna Reed Show") about what happens when we die. It is also a rare movie that recognizes the challenges children face when their parents re-marry.

Grant was in love with Loren while they were filming and there is enormous warmth and considerable sizzle between them onscreen. Reportedly he proposed to her and she turned him down just before the wedding scene was to be filmed.

Grant plays Tom Winters, a State Department official who travels a great deal on business, one reason he is estranged from his wife and three children. His wife dies and he comes back to Washington to find the children devastated and resentful. He takes them to a concert and the youngest one, Robert (Charles Herbert) runs away. He is found by Cinzia (Loren), who has also run away. Her father is the conductor of the Italian orchestra performing at the concert and she is tired of being cooped up in hotel rooms on the tour and never having any fun. When Tom meets Cinzia, he thinks she is a maid, and offers her the job of being housekeeper. She accepts, though it turns out she does not know anything about cooking or cleaning and the family ends up having to live on the leaky old contraption of the title. But the children love her.

The moment: Tom's late wife had a sister Carolyn (Martha Hyer), who has been taking care of the children. She wants to marry Tom and she is suspicious and jealous. She and her friends assume that Tom and Cinzia are sleeping together and they are condescending and rude. Carolyn tries to make Cinzia look common by giving her a nasty "gift," a dress that is very gaudy and cheap-looking.

Many movies have scenes where a horrible dress is transformed by tearing off some awful-looking trim, and this one is a great example. Of course, this dress benefits tremendously from being designed by the legendary Edith Head and worn by the gorgeous Sophia Loren, so don't try this at home.

More "it'll be fine if we just rip off this frou-frou" dress makeovers:

"Cinderella"

"My Favorite Wife"

"Bells are Ringin"

"True Lies"

§ § §

55

How Do You Know?
(2010)

The Proposal

The movie: Writer/director James L. Brooks makes two kinds of movies: great movies ("Terms of Endearment," "Broadcast News," "As Good as It Gets") and really interesting failures. Both have wonderfully messy characters, smart dialog, and captivating moments. "I'll Do Anything," originally shot as a musical, has a superb audition scene with Nick Nolte and some sharp humor and I'm still hopeful we get a director's cut with the songs restored someday. "Spanglish" has Adam Sandler's best performance and brilliant acting and the always-wonderful Téa Leoni. "How Do You Know?" has a lot wrong with it, but it is a really interesting mess.

Brooks says that his idea was a couple who meet on the worst day of both of their lives. Lisa (Reese Witherspoon) and George (Paul Rudd) meet just as each of them discovers that all of the dedication and integrity they brought to their jobs has not been enough to prevent collapse. Lisa has been cut from her professional softball team. George has discovered that he is being investigated by federal authorities for misrepresentation of financial reports - supplied by his father (Jack Nicholson), the company's CEO. And it is on that night that they go on a blind date that has them agreeing they would both be better off if they did not talk.

Rudd is especially good in this film. Watch him in the scene where George runs into Lisa in an elevator. His mouth has a cheery social smile but his eyes are sad and scared. And he is a rare actor who appears to think about what he is going to say before he speaks. But Nicholson's character is so poorly defined that he throws the movie off-balance.

The moment: Many, many movies have climactic proposals of marriage. But it is typical of the off-beat approach taken by Brooks that while the proposal in this movie is one of the most romantic in movie history, it does not involve the couple at the center of the story. Indeed, the man who makes the proposal is only in that one scene.

George's father has a loyal secretary named Annie, played by the always-excellent Kathryn Hahn. She is a single woman about to have a baby. One night, as Lisa has come to George's apartment to talk to him, he gets a call that Annie's son has been born and they go to the hospital to see her.

Al, the baby's father (Lenny Venito) shows up, hands George a movie camera, and tells Annie that the only reason he has not proposed to her is that he is out of a job and did not feel worthy. But he has realized that he can play an important role in her life by appreciating her and supporting her completely. George is so nonplussed that he forgets to hit record, so Al has to do it again, with George, Lisa, and Annie prompting him. It is sweet and tender and funny, and the kind of offbeat, non-linear story-construction that makes even Brooks' lesser films unmissable.

More great movie proposals:

"Love Actually"

"Walk the Line"

"The Runaway Bride"

"Jerry Maguire"

56

I Love You Again
(1940)

In the Woods

The movie: William Powell and Myrna Loy made more films together than any other couple since the silent era. Friends, not romantic partners, off-screen, they had an on-screen chemistry that was pure magic. They are most often associated with their six "Thin Man" films. Just as no one really cares about the mysteries in the "Thin Man" series, no one really cares that Nick Charles was not the Thin Man. Powell, always the most elegant and dapper of men, was not especially thin. The "thin man" was a character in the first film whose disappearance is investigated by former detective Nick Charles. We watch those films over and over because Powell and Loy were a rare on-screen married couple who were clearly crazy about each other but demonstrated it with an understated wit that was both sexy and sophisticated. I am very fond of the "Thin Man" series, especially the first one and "After the Thin Man" (with James Stewart). But I think that two of their other films are even better, "Libeled Lady" (co-starring Powell's real life love Jean Harlow) and "I Love You Again."

We meet Powell as a very un-Powell-esque drab, square, thoroughly middle-class man named Larry Wilson, sailing back to the United States following a business trip to Europe. He has bored his fellow passengers silly with his Babbit-y bromides and penny-pinching. But he is hit on the head and comes to as George Carey, a smooth con man whose last memory is of a train ride nine years before, when someone stole the money he was taking to bet on a fight. He has no recollection of his life as Larry, in a small town called Habersville. When he finds "Larry's" bankbook with a substantial balance, decides to visit Habersville to get as much of it as he can. What he does not expect is that Larry is married to Kay (Loy), and that he will be instantly smitten by her even though all she wants from him is a divorce.

Carey's horror as he finds out more and more about his life as Larry is balanced by Powell with smooth maneuvering to keep everyone from finding out that he can't remember anything about his life in Habersville. Loy is, as always, "the perfect wife" as she was often called for her movie portrayals. Kay is witty, wise and loyal -- she sees the essence of the truth about him and is adorably charmed by it.

Amnesia of this kind occurs only in the movies and soap operas. But it works because even though it makes no sense medically, it does make sense dramatically. When the suave con man Carey was hit on the head in a robbery nine years before, he became Larry, the boring businessman. It had to be because, at some level, a part of him wanted a "respectable life." At the end, he is neither Carey nor Larry, but a synthesis of both, ready to stay in Habersville with Kay and live happily ever after. Kay's motives are also justified. She married a bore like Larry because, as she says, she saw something exciting behind his eyes. She was the only one who glimpsed Carey inside of the stiff and proper Larry. And she also sees Carey at his best. When she says he is noble and honest, she turns out to be right.

The moment: All of this romance and meaning aside, the scene in the woods when "Larry" takes his Boy Rangers (including Carl Switzer, best known as "Alfalfa" from "Our Gang" and a very young Robert Blake) out for maneuvers in the woods is just plain wildly funny. Larry was an expert woodsman. Carey has no recollection of ever having seen a plant that wasn't potted. But his elaborate con game requires the sons of the town's wealthiest men to think there is undiscovered oil in the woods, so he must have everyone continue to think he is an expert Ranger leader. What happens is a small masterpiece of comic timing with slapstick set-pieces that move the plot (in both senses of the word) forward.

More from William Powell:

"My Man Godfrey"

"The Thin Man" series

"Mr. Roberts"

§ § §

57

INHERIT THE WIND
(1960)

Spencer Tracy Cross-Examines Frederic March

The movie: How do we know what we know? How do we decide what is true? These are the questions that are at the heart of the disputes we resolve through the law. The issue may be whether the light was green or red or whether the defendant reasonably believed the gun was loaded or whether the parties signed the contract, but we can only reach these questions by having some agreement about what "truth" is and how we determine it. Do we listen to our heads or our hearts? Do we believe what we are told, or do we challenge it, asking questions and evaluating the evidence? During some eras in history, trials were determined by tests of faith. Goat entrails were read to answer questions of fact. Those accused of witchery were dunked to see if they would prove their innocence by sinking. But our system is intended to determine the truth through logic and empiricism, even when the issue before the court is one of faith.

"Inherit the Wind," is based on the famous Scopes "monkey" trial, a 1925 case in which the two greatest lawyers in America went to court in Dayton, Tennessee. They argued what was then called the trial of the century. It was not about a famous crime. It wasn't even one of the lawsuits that changed American life, like Roe v. Wade or Brown v. the Board of Education. It was presented as a case about what we teach our children in school, but it was really about how we define ourselves. Nearly 100 years later, even Presidential candidates are still expected to take a position on this issue.

In the real-life case, a high school science teacher named John Scopes was charged with violating the state law that prohibited the teaching of Darwin's theories of evolution in public schools. The national headlines about Scopes' arrest brought the most famous orator of the day, three-time presidential candidate and President Wilson's Secretary of State, William Jennings Bryan, to Tennessee to argue for the prosecution. The most renowned trial lawyer in American history, Clarence Darrow, volunteered his services for the defense in his only pro bono appearance. For the movie, based on a play by Jerome Lawrence and Robert Lee, the names and some of the facts are changed, but some of the dialogue is taken directly from the transcripts of the Scopes trial.

In the first scene, the teacher is arrested in the presence of a clergyman and a man taking pictures. The leaders of the village discuss the pros and cons of prosecuting the case, which has led to newspaper stories across the country. Some are concerned that the prosecution will give the town a reputation for being contrary to "progress." Some stand firmly behind the law, one saying he would "rather have some heathens laughing at me than have my sons laughing at the Bible." When they hear that Matthew Harrison Brady (Fredric March playing the character based on William Jennings Bryan) has volunteered to come to Hillsboro to prosecute the case, they decide to accept. The merits of the law aside, Brady's presence will "fill up the town like a rain barrel in a thunderstorm," which is good for business. Brady's opponent will be Henry Drummond (Spencer Tracy playing the character based on Clarence Darrow).

The moment: The climax of the film comes when Drummond, not permitted to put his scientific experts on the stand, calls Brady as a witness as "one of the worlds foremost experts on the Bible and its teachings." Brady insists,

"Every word in this Bible should be accepted exactly as it is given there." When asked how the sun could stand still, Brady says that the same God who created natural law can change it. Drummond says that he thinks one thing is holy: "the individual human mind. In a child's power to master the multiplication table there is more sanctity than in all your shouted amens and holy holy hosannas. An idea is a greater monument than a cathedral, and the advance of man's knowledge is a greater miracle than all the sticks turned to snakes or the parting of the waters.... The Bible is a good book, but it is not the only book .... How do you know God didn't speak to Charles Darwin?" Drummond keeps pushing Brady about how he knows what he knows. In a key exchange, Brady refuses to consider the question: "I do not think about things I do not think about." Drummond responds, summarizing the theme of the case: "Do you ever think about things that you do think about?"

In this movie about skepticism, science, and faith, Drummond believes in one thing: the ability of the human mind to think, to question, and to know. While examining one of Cates' students during the trial he asks, "Did you believe everything Mr. Cates told you?" When the boy answers, "I don't know, I gotta think about it," Drummond responds, "Good for you! Good for you!" Drummond is not there on behalf of Darwin, and he is not there to argue against the Bible; he is there on behalf of open-mindedness and insistence on proof as the best way to honor the gifts of intelligence and curiosity. He leaves the courtroom holding both Darwin and the Bible.

More from Fredric March:

"The Best Years of Our Lives"

"Death of a Salesman"

"Nothing Sacred"

"Death Takes a Holiday"

"Design for Living"

58

It's Always Fair Weather
(1955)

Garbage Can Lid Dance

The movie: Gene Kelly's exuberantly athletic style made dancing look like a guy thing, and in some of his most memorable numbers he danced with other guys. In "On the Town" and "Take Me Out to the Ballgame" he danced with Frank Sinatra and Jules Munshin, top performers who were passable dancers. In this lesser-known film, Kelly's co-stars were not big names but they were sensational dancers and able to keep up with whatever co-choreographers Kelly and director Stanley Donen could dream up.

One was second-tier musical comedy performer Dan Dailey, Betty Grable's favorite co-star. The other, in a rare performance on screen, was Michael Kidd, one of the cinema's best choreographers, and the man behind the famous barn-raising dance in "Seven Brides for Seven Bothers." He was legendary for the strenuous physical challenge of his highly demanding dance numbers.

Unfortunately, the rest of the movie is not up to the same standard. Despite the best efforts of Betty Comden and Adolph Green ("Bells Are Ringing," "Singin' in the Rain") the characters and the satire of 1950's television do not hold up very well. The tunes from composer André Previn are pedestrian at best.

And there is an even bigger challenge. It was filmed in then-novel Cinemascope and it is very hard to see it as the director intended. The dance numbers take full advantage of the wide screen but television "pan and scan" showings slice off a third of the frame. It is well worth making the effort to see on a big screen, correctly proportioned, because these dances are magnificent.

It is the story of three soldiers who have been best pals and promise to keep in touch now that they are going home. As they say goodbye in their favorite hangout, they promise to reunite in exactly ten years.

Their lives do not work out the way they planned. Angie (Kidd) dreamed of owning a gourmet restaurant. Instead, he has a hamburger stand. Doug (Dailey) wanted to be an artist. But he is working in advertising, not the "Mad Men" era of cutthroat creativity and glamour but the high-pressure, ulcer-inducing, self-loathing world of producing jingles about dancing mops.

Ted (Kelly) dreamed of marrying his home-town sweetheart. But a "Dear John" letter as the movie begins dashes his hopes and he spends the decade partying, playing pool, and trying to make ends meet as a boxing promoter. They all show up for the big reunion but find they have nothing in common and do not even respect each other. Ultimately,

though, everything ends up happily with the help of a cheesy television program.

It is not necessary to watch the whole movie, though you don't want to miss Kelly's solo dance number on roller skates.

The moment: The show-stopper is in the first fifteen minutes, a dance number as the trio goes out on the town to help Ted get over his heartbreak. They do a drunken dance through the streets of New York that ends with their putting garbage can lids on their feet and using them as a sort of giant tap shoe.

Sublime.

More memorable roller skate movie moments:

Fred Astaire and Ginger Rogers in "Shall We Dance"

Barbra Streisand in "Funny Girl"

Charlie Chaplin in "The Rink"

Bow Wow and the gang in "Roll Bounce"

Olivia Newton John in "Xanadu"

§ § §

59

IT'S A MAD MAD MAD MAD WORLD (1963)

Saul Bass Opening Titles

The movie: "It's a Mad Mad Mad Mad World" has just about every comic actor in Hollywood plus Spencer Tracy in a story about a wild race to find the buried treasure: $350,000 in stolen money, creating chaos in every relationship and by every possible mode of transportation along the way. It is wild, silly fun and highly recommended for the sheer pleasure of seeing a movie that includes top comedy performers from television, vaudeville, movies, and theater, with cameos from comedy greats like Jerry Lewis and the Three Stooges. Mickey Rooney, Sid Caesar, Buddy Hackett, Phil Silvers, Edie Adams, and Ethel Merman are among those trying to get to the money before anyone else and Tracy and William Demerest are the cops who have been trying to find the stolen money for 15 years.

This was one of the films lucky enough to have an opening title sequence by Saul Bass, a graphic designer and filmmaker responsible for many instantly recognizable corporate logos and movie posters and for the award-winning short film "Why Man Creates," but best remembered for his small gems that opened films by directors like Alfred Hitchcock, Otto Preminger, and Martin Scorsese.

The opening credits are more than a way to let the audience know who made the film while they are settling into their seats. It is a "visual overture," in the words of producer Walter Parkes, an introduction to the movie's tone and themes, an invitation into the world the movie will create. They can be an art form all their own. More people can describe the opening credits for the first "Pink Panther" movie than can tell you the names of the actors who appeared in it. The music by Henry Mancini and the cartoon by Friz Freleng and partner David H. DePatie were spun off into a series of their own.

These days most opening sequences are live action, and some are very creative. I loved seeing the characters dancing together at over the opening credits of "Deliver Us from Eva," and the very different tone set by the opening dance in "Do the Right Thing." The title sequence of "Juno," designed by Gareth Smith and Jenny Lee, was impressionistic and evocative in combining live action and animation to introduce us to the title character. But no one does it better than Saul Bass, the best known and most influential of title sequence artists. Steven Spielberg's "Catch Me If You Can" has animated opening credits created by Parisians Olivier Kuntzel and Florence Deygas that pay tribute to Bass' style, in part because the movie is set in the era when most of the movies Bass worked on were released.

The moment: "It's a Mad Mad Mad Mad World" presented Bass with quite a challenge: dozens of names. The contracts of movie stars often spell out in great detail the size, placement, and order of their names in the credits. The enormous cast of very big stars could have led to an opening title sequence that looked like a page in the telephone book. But Bass made it into an advantage, using each list of names to help convey something about the comedy that was coming. It begins with a simple red frame, the score by Ernest Gold sounding like a slightly off-kilter circus. A little animated man in black carries out an enormous globe, which topples him over. Then a saw starts poking out of the globe and cuts out a square. A hand reaches out holding a flag with the name of the movie's biggest star, Spencer Tracy. A hand comes down to nail the globe shut again and the fight is on. The globe is opened like a tuna can and more names tumble out, "in alphabetical order," but they start scrambling over each other to be on top of the list. The globe bounces like a ball, cracks open like an egg, and gets ridden like a unicycle. We get information but more importantly, we get a sense of the mad mad world that we are about to enter.

More classic opening titles from Saul Bass:

"Anatomy of a Murder"

"North By Northwest"

"Vertigo"

"Psycho"

"The Shining"

"The Man with the Golden Arm"

§ § §

60

The Lady Eve
(1941)

Mirror Image

The movie: Writer/director Preston Sturges was one of Hollywood's most singular talents. He made half a dozen screwball comedy classics with an inimitable (though many have tried to imitate it) combination of the wildest farce and the wittiest dialog. The Coen brothers movie "O Brother Where Art Thou" is one of many tributes to Sturges by other filmmakers. Its title comes from "Sullivan's Travels," with Joel McCrea as a successful Hollywood director of silly comedies with titles like "So Long Sarong" who wants to make a serious film about the Depression called "O Brother Where Art Thou." He never does, because he learns that he can make a greater contribution by making audiences laugh. Sturges himself decided to try to make a serious film, "The Great Moment," but as with his later comedies, it was not successful.

"The Lady Eve" is the story of a con woman who falls for her mark, but with a twist only Sturges could devise. Barbara Stanwyck plays Jean Harrington, who travels with her father (the great Charles Coburn), making their way by cheating at cards and other small-time scams. On a ship back to the United States from South America, they meet Charles Pike (Henry Fonda), heir to an ale fortune, who has been studying snakes up the Amazon. He falls for Jean until he learns the truth about her past. Determined to get revenge for his leaving her, she re-appears as "Lady Eve Sidwich" to fleece him all over again. And he falls for her once more -- literally and repeatedly -- in a very funny scene at his parents' home.

Harvard professor Stanley Cavell's book, *Pursuits of Happiness: The Hollywood Comedy of Remarriage*, is one of the most thoughtful and purely delightful books on movies I know. He has identified a category of film that includes "Adam's Rib," "His Girl Friday," "My Favorite Wife," "The Philadelphia Story," and this one that he calls "comedies of remarriage" because they involve people who have already been married. These stories are especially compelling because it is much more meaningful to fall in love with someone you already know and have seen at their worst than with someone with whom you are still in the dewy-eyed stage of romantic illusion. He points out that the foundation for this light romantic comedy is in the themes of transformation and recognition that go back to Shakespeare and beyond that back to ancient myth and the Bible (note the name of the female lead and the movie's advertising tagline: "Eve sure knew her apples"). In one of my favorite passages in the book he says that while in Shakespeare the young lovers often go to magical woods or other less inhabited places to sort out their problems, in movies of this genre they usually go to Connecticut.

The moment: It is the first night on board the ship and all of the eligible females are on the lookout for Pike. A typical screenwriter might let us see Pike come into the dining room and pass through the obstacle course of young women trying their various stratagems to get his attention. But Sturges always has his own special view. And, it turns out, so does Eve. In a camera trick that was very innovative for its time, Sturges shows us the scene through the mirror in Eve's make-up compact, which she is using to watch what is going on while she delivers a sports-commentator-style commentary to show us that she is way ahead of the others. What we will see is that she and Pike are going through the looking-glass to a mirror-world where the trickster is the tricked and the one who pretends not to be in love falls even deeper.

More from Preston Sturges:

"Sullivan's Travels"

"The Palm Beach Story"

"Miracle of Morgan's Creek"

"Christmas in July"

"The Great McGinty"

§ § §

61

Lars and the Real Girl
(2007)

Casseroles

The movie: A repressed man in the frozen Northwest named Lars (Ryan Gosling) falls in love with a life-sized sex toy (the "real girl") named Bianca, and this tender treasure of a film makes his story (it almost feels right to say "their story") very sweet and even romantic. But the film, which won a Humanitas prize for promoting human dignity, meaning, and freedom, is not about Lars. The heart of the film in every way is the community around him and the sensitivity and grace of their support.

Lars lives in a tiny cabin behind the house where he grew up, now occupied by his brother Gus (Paul Schneider) and his pregnant wife Karin (Emily Mortimer). He works in a cubicle and goes to church and is polite to everyone but he stays mostly to himself and turns down Karin's frequent invitations to eat with them. And then, one day, he accepts a dinner invitation and tells Karin he is bringing a girlfriend he met online. She is overjoyed, until he shows up with Bianca. Gus and Karin are too stunned to do anything but play along. They take him to the local doctor, Dagmar (Patricia Clarkson), who soberly takes Bianca's blood pressure and tells Lars he must bring her in for treatments every week as a way of getting him to come talk with her.

There is a lovely scene where Gus and Karin come to the members of the church who run things in the town to try to get them to go along with Lars' delusion. One of them is hesitant: "We don't want anything to do with her. She is a 'golden calf.' We all know what happened with that." But another reminds the group that everyone has something a bit odd or embarrassing. "These things happen. Lars is a good boy." When he brings her to church in a wheelchair, everyone greets Bianca warmly.

First-time screenwriter Nancy Oliver (HBO's "Six Feet Under" and "True Blood") called the story "a contemporary fairy tale" that explores "the geography of kindness and compassion." We learn in Lars' sessions with Dagmar about the source of the crushing internal pressure that led to his delusion. But we learn from the gentle grace of those around him how and why he will come back from it. The more they accept Bianca (she gets a job, reads to the children at school, and is even elected to the school board), the more Lars is able to let go of her.

Finally, at Bianca's funeral, the pastor says, "From her wheelchair, Bianca reached out and touched us all. In ways we could have never imagined. She was a teacher. She was a lesson in courage. And Bianca loved us all. Especially Lars. Especially him."

The moment: Bianca is like a child's transition object. Lars holds onto her until he works through his separation anxiety and then it is time to let her go. Lars tells Gus and Karin that Bianca is very sick. Karin by this point is so committed to what Bianca has brought to his life that she is the one who does not want Lars to give her up. But they take her to the hospital, and then they go home. The good ladies of the town are there. They bring casseroles and their needlework. "That's what people do when tragedy strikes," one explains. "They come over and sit."

It is a lot easier for a movie to show callousness and cruelty than to show kindness and it is very rare to show kindness that preserves the dignity of the person on the receiving end. The simple goodness of the statement made by being there and the actual words used is in its inclusiveness. It is not just that they respect the very real tragedy of Bianca's loss enough to be there. It is their gentle reminder to Lars that he is a part of a community where people come over and sit when people are sad to let them know they are not alone.

More Ryan Gosling:

"The Slaughter Rule"

"The Believer"

"Stay"

"Half Nelson"

"Drive"

§ § §

62

THE LAST WALTZ
(1978)

The Broken Guitar Strap

The movie: When they played with Bob Dylan, he just called them "the band." And so, when they began to perform on their own, they took that as their name. The roots rock group included Rick Danko, Levon Helm, Robbie Robertson, Garth Hudson, and Richard Manuel. When they decided to stop touring, Martin Scorsese made a documentary film about their final performance after sixteen years on the road. The concert was held on Thanksgiving Day 1976, at the Winterland Ballroom in San Francisco and it featured some of The Band's musical friends and influences including some of the biggest names in rock and roll and other genres: Paul Butterfield, Eric Clapton, Neil Diamond, Bob Dylan, Emmylou Harris, Ronnie Hawkins, Dr. John, Joni Mitchell, Van Morrison, Ringo Starr, Muddy Waters, Ronnie Wood, Bobby Charles and Neil Young.

This epic concert gave Scorsese hours of great footage to sift through. A true lover of rock n' roll as well as a fan of songwriter and front man for The Band, Robbie Robertson, Scorsese combined interviews and poignant exchanges between veterans of the road with brilliant rock music for what many consider the best concert film ever made. It is filled with beautifully observed moments that are musically thrilling and also provide meaningful insights into what it means to love music so completely and love performing almost as much. It is clear how moved they are by each other, and it is deeply touching.

The moment: The concert was well under way when guitar legends Eric Clapton and Robbie Robertson took to the stage. The roar from the audience began to swell in anticipation of dueling guitar performances by two great musicians serenading each other, challenging each other, and bringing out the best in each other. Scorsese and Director of Photography Michael Chapman show us the appreciative smiles and fond expressions on the faces of Clapton and Robertson as they watch each other perform. As their song, "Somewhere Down The Road" races into the home stretch, you can see arms waving in the audience and people bouncing up and down with sheer exhilaration.

And then, in the midst of the grand space of the 5400-seat ballroom, we see a private moment between them, a silent exchange between two master musicians with decades of public performances behind them, unobserved by the audience but captured by Scorsese's cameras.

As Clapton was beginning his solo, his guitar unexpectedly slips from its strap. He stops mid-note and clutches at his guitar to keep it from crashing to the floor. In all the pandemonium on stage, nobody else recognizes what was happening but Robertson, who had been playing back-up to Clapton's solo, instantly assesses the problem. Without missing a beat, he picks up the lead with a spontaneous, dazzling guitar riff. His impromptu solo dominates the stage as the spotlight searches to find who is playing and Clapton turns his back to the audience to re-attach his strap. As Robertson plays, he monitors Clapton's progress out of the corner of his eye. When the strap is back on, Robertson seamlessly returns to the background and Clapton resumes where he had left off.

The best thing about watching musicians perform is the way they look at each other while they play, the absolute focus they have on the music and the performance and their ability to communicate without words about what is going on. This moment shows us the near-telepathy between musicians playing together. It shows how Robertson responds as a musician and as a performer, able to pick up in a split second and finish his contribution to let Clapton continue seamlessly without letting the audience know that it was anything but planned that way.

More great concert films:

"Stop Making Sense"

"Rust Never Sleeps"

"Woodstock"

"Monterey Pop"

"Shine a Light"

"U2 3D"

§ § §

63

A LEAGUE OF THEIR OWN
(1992)

Playing in a Different League

The movie: The whole storyline about the competition between the two sisters played by Geena Davis and Lori Petty is snooze-worthy, but the movie around it is so fresh and engaging that it almost does not matter. This is the story of the All-American Girls Professional Baseball League (AAGPBL), a sort of sports version of Rosie the Riveter. With the men off fighting World War II, baseball owners decided to set up a women's league, and here it is presented as a liberating experience for women who otherwise would have had no opportunities for a career or travel or a chance to see what they could achieve as athletes. In one scene Rosie O'Donnell, as one of the Rockford Peaches, explains that she put up with boyfriends who treated her badly because she always thought there was something wrong with her. Now that she has found that there are other women like her and that there is a place where what she can do is considered valuable, she can never allow anyone to diminish her that way again.

There are dozens of wonderful moments in this film. Tom Hanks gives one of his best performances as a onetime star player turned alcoholic who is assigned to coach the Peaches but pays no attention to them until he realizes that they are true baseball players. His line, "There's no crying in baseball" is justifiably listed as number 54 on the American Film Institute's list of the top movie quotes of all time. Madonna, Garry Marshall, Jon Lovitz, and O'Donnell are marvelous.

It is clear that the actresses themselves, like the women they portray, are liberated by the opportunity to use their strength as well as their beauty. And it is lovely to see the real veterans of the league playing over the closing credits.

The moment: In the midst of all of the girl power good feelings, there is a wrenching moment that kicks the entire film into a higher dimension. The players are practicing, when they notice some other women watching them. They are black. When one of them throws the ball and they see how good she is, they exchange a nod of respect and acknowledgement that there are still a lot of barriers to cross.

More about the early days of baseball:

"Nine Men Out"

"The Bingo Long Traveling All-Stars & Motor Kings"

"Soul of the Game"

§ § §

64

THE LITTLE COLONEL
(1935)

Two Superstars on the Stairs in the Movies' First Inter-racial DanceTeam

The movie: Bill "Bojangles" Robinson was the most admired dancer of the vaudeville era. Shirley Temple was the only child ever to become the top box office star of her time. And in an era where laws still enforced the separation of the races, they became the first integrated couple to dance together on film.

Robinson and Temple appeared together in four movies. "The Little Colonel" was their first. While it reflects the racism of the era in which it was made and the racism of the post-Civil War era in which it was set, the interaction between the two superstars is still enchanting.

The plot, based on a book by Annie Fellows Johnston, is strictly second-rate *Little Lord Fauntleroy,* but then most Shirley Temple movies have pretty much the same story: her irrepressible sunniness brings about a reconciliation between some grumpy grown-ups. In this case, the crusty grandfather is played by Lionel Barrymore. He disowned his daughter for marrying a Yankee. The granddaughter played by Shirley (dubbed "The Little Colonel" because she has disarmingly won the hearts of a military regiment) has inherited his flinty determination. You can guess the rest, including Robinson's role as a servant.

Robinson began dancing for money when he was a child, though he did not become a star until he was well into his adult years. The movie "Harlem in Heaven" and the bittersweet song "Mr. Bojangles" are inspired by his life story. He stars in another film inspired by his life, "Stormy Weather," with "Cabin in the Sky" among the very few films that feature the top African-American performers of the era. One of his trademarks was the stair-step dance, which he claimed he invented as he was about to receive an honor from the King of England, who was standing at the top of the stairs.

Temple was the biggest star in the world when she was just six years old. She later went into politics and served in both Republican and Democratic administrations as Ambassador and Chief of Protocol.

The moment: Robinson plays the butler to the old man. He befriends the granddaughter and shows her his special dance. Two of the biggest stars of their time, half a century apart in age, hold hands and dance up the stairs, having a wonderful time -- until cranky Lionel Barrymore comes in

to stop them.

Robinson and Temple danced together again in "Rebecca of Sunnybrook Farm," "The Littlest Rebel," and "Just Around the Corner."

More Shirley Temple:

"Heidi"

"Poor Little Rich Girl"

"Wee Willie Winkie"

"Captain January"

More Bill Robinson:

"Stormy Weather"

"Up the River"

"Rebecca of Sunnybrook Farm"

§ § §

65

LITTLE MISS SUNSHINE (2006)

Talking to Dwayne

The movie: "Little Miss Sunshine" is the quintessential indie darling, a hit at Sundance that became an Oscar-winning box office success. The story behind it feels like a "they said it couldn't be done" indie itself. It had a screenplay from Michael Arndt, a former assistant to Matthew Broderick, who went on to write "Toy Story 3"). It also had first-time feature film co-directors Valerie Faris and Jonathan Drayton, and a five-year struggle to get made. That experience informed the movie's themes as the characters all reconsider their ideas about what constitutes success.

When the family in this movie learns that their van cannot be repaired in time for them to get to the Little Miss Sunshine competition, they decide to drive it as is. And that means that in order to get it to start, they all have to get out and push, then chase after it and jump in. And so when they have to stop for food or gas or adolescent meltdown or illness or being pulled over by a cop, even when they are miserable and furious with each other, they all have to get out and push together and then run and jump inside. And every time that happens, all of them laugh and feel somehow proud and happy and connected.

All of them means: Richard (Greg Kinnear), the father, a motivational speaker and writer who knows everything about winning except that he hasn't been able to actually succeed at anything, Sheryl (Toni Collette), the mother, who is doing her best to hold everyone together, including her brother, Frank (Steve Carrell), who recently attempted suicide over the loss of his lover to the second-most important Proust scholar in the country (he is the first), teenage son Dwayne (Paul Dano), who has taken a vow of silence because, as he explains in writing, he hates everyone, Grandpa, Richard's father (Oscar-winner Alan Arkin), who got kicked out of the nursing home for profanity and heroin-snorting, and of course Olive (Abigail Breslin), the Little Miss Sunshine contestant herself.

"Everybody just pretend to be normal, okay?" begs Richard, as a highway patrolman pulls them over. But what is great about this family is that, while they are far from the idealized notions of normality presented in television commercials and Hallmark cards, they are in fact very normal. Sometimes that works better for them than others. Richard's most "normal" quality is his effort to be normal, to succeed in conventional terms. His desperate attempt to think of himself as not only successful but as someone who can define success for others as a career is a reflection of the American spirit, its unquenchable hope, ambition, and belief in the future. Sheryl has a different kind of unquenchable hope. She is not convinced that Richard knows what he is doing and she is not always able to live up to her own expectations, but she is clear about her dedication to her family and to providing the support that they need.

Most of the movie has these characters all together interacting with each other, often noisily. It is well written both in dialog and structure, with surprising depth and complexity. Dano's performance as the silent Dwayne is one of the great anchoring strengths of the movie, and there are a couple of quietly powerful moments with him and just one other member of the family. One is when he and Frank sit on a dock while Olive and her parents are at the pageant getting ready. Frank tells Dwayne about Proust.

Total loser. Never had a real job. Unrequited love affairs. Gay. Spent 20 years writing a book almost no one reads. But he's also probably the greatest writer since Shakespeare. Anyway, he uh... he gets down to the end of his life, and he looks back and decides that all those years he suffered, those were the best years of his life, 'cause they made him who he was. All those years he was happy? You know, total waste. Didn't learn a thing. So, if you sleep until you're 18... Ah, think of the suffering you're gonna miss. I mean high school? High school-those are your prime suffering years. You don't get better suffering than that.

The moment: Dwayne learns that he is color-blind and therefore will not be able to become an Air Force pilot, as he had hoped. The first sound we hear from him in the movie is a moan of utter anguish as he runs out of the van, inconsolable. The adults look after him helplessly. But his little sister, Olive, walks over to him and gently puts her hand on his shoulder without saying a word. His silence was isolating. Hers is inexpressibly eloquent.

More Steve Carell:

"Dan in Real Life"

"Date Night"

"Anchorman"

§ § §

66

LOVE WITH THE PROPER STRANGER (1963)

Chick Flick Triple Threat Apology

The movie: My husband says that the most important requirement for a "chick flick" is the presence of at least one apology, with extra points if it is (a) in public and (b) includes a marriage proposal. He is right that apologies are a recurring theme in movies that appeal to women. While both genders like movies that show us a character arc, with the hero or heroine learning some important lessons, often by making mistakes, male audiences still tend to see the apology as a form of submission while women see it as a form of inclusion.

This lovely black and white film from director Robert Mulligan ("To Kill a Mockingbird") and screenwriter Arnold Schulman ("A Hole in the Head," "Tucker: A Man and His Dream") has an intimate, documentary feel and a little a grit in its New York setting in contrast to the stylized, high-gloss romantic comedies of the era, like those starring Doris Day. Natalie Wood plays Angie, a sheltered girl from an Italian family who, as the movie begins, contacts musician Rocky Papasano (Steve McQueen) to tell him that she is pregnant.

For Angie, their one-time encounter was a brief moment of rebellion. She had never done anything like that before. For Rocky, Angie was one of many. He has been careful not to get tied down. She does not want to tie him down, now. They hardly know one another. All she wants from him is help in getting a then-illegal abortion.

Rocky does as she asks, but tells her that she does not have to go through with it. She thinks she is determined, but at the last moment, finds that she cannot do it. Angie's brother finds out and insists Rocky marry Angie. Rocky is willing. But Angie does not want a shotgun wedding. She wants "bells and banjos." If Rocky cannot marry her for love, she would rather marry the shy restaurateur (Tom Bosley) who is willing to raise the child as his own.

We know all along that Rocky and Angie are meant to be together, but it is a pleasure to see them figure it out. "I don't know what it is," Rocky says to Angie as they try to have a belated normal dinner date. "First time in my life I come to see a girl, I feel like I'm 14 years old. Even when I was 14, I didn't feel like that." He charmingly picks up on her habit of speaking in the third person about what is going on ("look how surprised he sounds!"). But he insists that he does not want a steady job. Although he is jealous of her relationship to the other man, he cannot bring himself to let her know that he cares about her. She throws him out of her apartment, telling him, "You're dead!"

The moment: That is where the triple-threat apology comes in. Commuters clog the streets at the end of the day as Angie comes out of Macy's. At first, she hardly notices that there is a crowd, and then all she can see is the sign: "Better wed than dead."

And then she hears the banjo and bells, and then she sees that it is Rocky, his way of letting her know that he is sorry, that he loves her, and that he wants to make a life with her and their baby. Mulligan pulls back the camera and they get lost in the crowd of New Yorkers on their way home after a day at work.

More from Natalie Wood:

    "West Side Story"

    "Rebel Without a Cause"

    "Splendor in the Grass"

    "The Great Race"

§ § §

67

THE MAGNIFICENT AMBERSONS (1942)

The Story of the Indian Girl

The movie: Orson Welles co-wrote, directed, and starred in "Citizen Kane," a movie that has appeared on top of more "greatest of all time" lists than any other film, all before he turned 26. He then spent the rest of his career trying to get the money and authority to make another movie without studio interference. It never happened. But films like "The Third Man," "Touch of Evil," "The Trial," "The Lady From Shanghai" and "F for Fake" are all arresting, with stunning images, striking imagination, and moments of singular brilliance.

Anyone who loves film cherishes the dream that someday the definitive Orson Welles version of "The Magnificent Ambersons" will be found. This was his second film, made with some of the same people he worked with on "Citizen Kane," including editor Robert Wise and actors Agnes Moorehead, Ray Collins, and Joseph Cotton. It is based on Booth Tarkington's Pulitzer Prize-winning novel about a wealthy family whose fortunes dwindle as the industrialists of the 20th century take over. The movie focuses on George (Tim Holt), the spoiled heir of a wealthy and prominent Indiana family. He gets his "comeuppance" when everything he takes for granted as his birthright is taken from him.

Welles completed a 135-minute version that was butchered by the movie studio and issued with a tacked-on ending. Even so, it is a marred masterpiece. The settings by Albert

S. D'Agostin and the cinematography by Stanley Cortez are gorgeously evocative in the early, nostalgic scenes and bleakly dismal after George loses everything. The sequences of the sleigh ride and the ball are breathtaking.

The moment: Joseph Cotton plays Eugene, who loved George's mother when they were young and tries to renew their acquaintance when they are both widowed. George selfishly interferes because he does not want his mother to remarry.

Anne Baxter plays Eugene's daughter, who is fond of George but realizes that he is too selfish and immature for a relationship. There is a scene of enormous poignancy as the father and daughter go for a walk and she tells him a bittersweet story about an (imaginary) Indian legend. It is clear to both of them and to us that it is their way of talking about their feelings. It is taken almost verbatim from the Tarkington novel, but feels intimate and improvised.

Lucy: Ever hear the Indian name for that little grove of beech trees?

Eugene: No, and you never did either. Well?

Lucy: The name was Loma-Nashah. It means: "They-couldn't-help-it."

Eugene: Doesn't sound like it.

Lucy: Indian names don't. There was a bad Indian chief, the worst Indian that ever lived, and his name was...it was Vendonah. Means: "Rides-Down-Everything."

Eugene: What?

Lucy: His name was Vendonah, same thing as: "Rides-Down-Everything."

Eugene: I see. [She laughs] Go on.

Lucy: Vendonah was unspeakable. He was so proud he wore iron shoes and walked over people's faces. So at last, the tribe decided that it wasn't a good enough excuse for him that he was young and inexperienced. He'd have to go. So they took him down to the river, put him in a canoe, and pushed him out from shore. The current carried him on down to the ocean. And he never got back. They didn't want him back, of course. They hated Vendonah, but they weren't able to discover any other warrior they wanted to make chief in his place. They couldn't help feeling that way.

Eugene: I see. So that's why they named the place: "They-couldn't help-it."

Lucy: Must have been.

Eugene: So you're going to stay in your garden. You think it's better just to keep walking about among your flowerbeds and get old like a pensive garden lady in a Victorian engraving? Huh?

Lucy: I suppose I'm like that tribe that lived here, Papa. I had too much unpleasant excitement. I don't want any more. In fact, I don't want anything but you.

Eugene: You don't? What was the name of that grove?

Lucy: "They-could…"

Eugene: No, the Indian name, I mean.

Lucy: Oh. Mola-Haha. [They laugh together]

Eugene: Mola-Haha. That wasn't the name you said.

Lucy: Oh, I've forgotten.

Eugene: So you have. Perhaps you remember the chief's name better?

Lucy: I don't.

Eugene: I hope some day you can forget it.

"Citizen Kane" has a similarly poignant scene, a speech by Mr. Bernstein about the girl in the white dress.

More Joseph Cotton:
- "Citizen Kane"
- "Shadow of a Doubt"
- "The Third Man"
- "Gaslight"

§ § §

68

Manhunter (1986)

The Lady and the Tiger

The movie: For me, the real Hannibal Lecter will always be Brian Cox in "Manhunter" (spelled "Lecktor" in this film), stylishly directed by Michael Mann. Sir Anthony Hopkins created one of the most memorable villains in film history and it is a mesmerizing, iconic performance. But I love the more understated and believable version of the character in the first movie based on the serial killer novels by Thomas Harris. It was later remade with Hopkins under the original title of the book, "Red Dragon."

As in "Silence of the Lambs," Lecktor is in prison, consulted by an FBI criminal profiler investigating another serial killer. Will Graham (William Peterson) is in retirement after capturing Lecktor. Physically and emotionally damaged by that case and vulnerable because of the same sensitivity that makes him so good at understanding killers and anticipating their next moves, he has promised himself and his family he will not go back.

At first, when he is asked to return to track down a new serial killer called The Tooth Fairy, he says he will only examine the evidence. He will not do the investigation. But when he finds out that The Tooth Fairy has been communicating with Lecktor and that they have a mutual interest in Graham himself, he is once again drawn into the investigation.

He visits Lecktor in prison. Cox's performance is not as showy as Sir Anthony's but it is every bit as disturbing. Mann made a conscious decision to keep Lecktor's time on screen to a minimum, saying that he was "such a charismatic character that I wanted the audience almost not to get enough of him."

We know who the killer is before Graham does. It is Francis Dollarhyde (Tom Noonan), who works in a photo lab, where he sees the pictures of the families he will select as his victims.

The moment: Reba McClane (Joan Allen) is a blind woman who also works in the photo lab. Dollarhyde brings her to the zoo, where a tiger has been sedated, and so for the first time she can "see" what the big, powerful creature looks like by touching him. The look on Allen's face as she touches the tiger's soft fur, powerful muscles, and huge, sharp teeth shows us her amazement, her pleasure in learning what this creature is like and in the pure sensuality of being close to such a magnificent animal, her thrill at being able to get close to the creature who would be so terrifying if he were awake.

Allen, who studied at the New York Institute for the Blind to prepare for the role, not only learned about how a blind person moves and experiences the world through touch and sound; she observed the way that some blind people are unusually expressive and unrestrained in their facial expressions because they have never observed the way sighted people try to maintain control to keep their feelings to themselves. Her face, as she touches the tiger is heart-wrenchingly open.

Dollarhyde, who earlier had pushed her hand away when she wanted to touch his face, almost swoons with emotion as he watches her. It is clear that he longs for her even more. Now that he knows she is open to the wildness of the tiger, he can almost believe she might understand the wildness in him. This is a gorgeous moment that works on many levels, pure visual splendor, psychological insight and narrative development, and the metaphors of the temporarily sedated wildness in both animal and human.

The remake, "Red Dragon," with Emma Watson, also has a sedated tiger scene and it is very good, but the original is better.

More movie serial killers:

"Se7en"

"Psycho"

"Time After Time"

§ § §

69

THE MAN WHO SHOT LIBERTY VALANCE (1962)

Might, Right, and Reason

The movie: No one has done more than director John Ford to form our notion of the 19th century American West and indeed our notion of the intrepid and independent American spirit. While he made enduring films with other settings, Ford's western movies, many starring John Wayne, showed us the flinty, independent pioneers in the vastness of Monument Valley, facing the challenges of reconciling the needs of pioneer communities during the era of Westward expansion with the vast expanses of the natural world and its Native American residents. "My Darling Clementine" (about the gunfight at the OK Corral), "Fort Apache," "Stagecoach," and "The Searchers" reveal our past and put our present struggles in context as we continue to build on the best of our history and work toward greater understanding.

"The Man Who Shot Liberty Valance" deals with the grandest and most profound themes of the human condition, packaged in the guise of a shoot-em-up western melodrama. Like "The Magnificent Ambersons," it deals with the poignancy and of old ways gradually disintegrating in favor of the new and the impact on heroes whose contribution is no longer needed. Like "Friendly Persuasion" and "Charlie Wilson's War," it deals with the choice between reasoned civilization and raw power as the best response to evil. Like "Amadeus," it deals with the falsity of worldly recognition, and the unfair gap between fame and fortune on one hand,

and true accomplishment on the other. Like "Citizen Kane," it deals with the hollowness of coming to the end of your life and recognizing that you've been living a lie. And like "Casablanca," it deals with a love triangle where a woman is torn between her love for an important and accomplished man and her love for a brooding loner.

"The Man Who Shot Liberty Valance" is not as cerebral as more esteemed "art" films, but it has plenty of heart and moral heft. Part of the greatness of director John Ford was his ability to decoct such themes to their essence, using simple vocabulary of the Wild West and expressing conflicts as directly as a shootout on a town's single street. The violence in his films is effectively staged but more important, it is a meaningful part of the story.

The moment: There is no better example of this than the confrontation in the cafe. James Stewart plays Ransom Stoddard, a young and idealistic lawyer who arrives in the small town of Shinbone to bring civilization, education and the rule of law. Upon his arrival he is beaten and robbed by the outlaw Liberty Valance (Lee Marvin), who terrorizes the town with impunity. Only one man is tougher and a better shot than Liberty Valance: horse rancher Tom Doniphon (John Wayne).

While Stoddard recuperates from his beating, he is forced to take a job waiting on tables and working in the kitchen of the local café. Doniphin is seated in the cafe when Valance and his gang come in to eat. When Stoddard appears in the kitchen doorway wearing an apron and carrying trays, the cast of characters for the morality play is complete: the unreasoning evil Valance, the symbol of civilization Stoddard, and in the corner the embodiment of power, Wayne, watching like a hawk. At first Stoddard attempts to avoid a confrontation. Taking a deep breath, he tries to walk past his tormentor to deliver food to another table. But Valance won't have it. He sticks out his foot and trips Stoddard, sending him and the food tumbling to the floor while the beautiful heroine watched. The emasculation of reason is complete.

But Valance's laughter is cut short when Doniphon stands up and announces that the tray on the floor was carrying his dinner. Valance has insulted Stoddard, but he has also insulted Doniphon, who demands that Valance pick up the food. The tide has turned. Now it's Valance's turn to try to avoid conflict. Valance's sidekick stoops down to pick up the food for him, squealing, "I'll get it, Liberty!" but Doniphon will have none of it. Doniphon kicks the stooge out of the way without even looking in his direction, steps closer to Valance and through clenched teeth says evenly but with meaning, "I said you, Liberty. You pick it up." The virility of ethical non-cognitivism has never been more effectively portrayed on the screen.

Later, Stoddard will build his career on having killed Valance, knowing that it was really Doniphon. But Stoddard can use that fame to help the community with his education and willingness to work within the system to obtain statehood for the territory while Doniphon would not, and he does not want the intrusion that would come with taking credit. Both are necessary to forge the communities of the West. Stoddard was willing to speak up publicly to oppose Valance even at the risk of his own life. Doniphon had the skill and the courage to be the man who shot Liberty Valance, and to let someone else take the credit and use it to benefit the community, understanding that "civilization" would impinge on his stature and rugged individualism.

At the end of his career, after Doniphon's death, Stoddard tries to set the record straight, but he is memorably told, "When the legend becomes the fact, print the legend." Ford knew he was doing that, too, and wanted us to know it.

More from John Wayne:

"Rio Lobo"

"The Quiet Man"

"True Grit"

§ § §

70

MEET ME IN ST. LOUIS (1944)

Gloves

The movie: This glorious musical is based on the childhood of writer Sally Benson. She was best known during her lifetime for her "Junior Miss" series of stories about a modern teenager, but her most enduring legacy is this episodic portrayal of the life of a comfortably middle-class family in the year leading up to the opening of the 1904 World's Fair in St. Louis. Director Vincent Minnelli was already in love with his star, Judy Garland, and he did everything he could to show her at her best, almost as if the camera was in love with her, too. She introduced three of her signature songs, "The Boy Next Door," "The Trolley Song," and "Have Yourself a Merry Little Christmas."

It is a loving and nostalgic look at a time of innocence and optimism, where a long-distance call was almost as thrilling as the World's Fair. One of the movie's most evocative scenes is Halloween, celebrated very differently in those days, but like today the one night of the year where children have the power to frighten the grown-ups.

This is one of the most loving of all movie families. Everyone in it treats all of the other members with trust and affection, even, when it comes to the youngest, indulgence. They are interested in each other and supportive of each other, whether it is the seasoning of a sauce, the filling of a dance card, or facilitating an engagement. While the family does not support the father when his job requires him to move to

New York, but that is in part a reflection of their devotion to the life they have together in St. Louis, as well as a wished-for outcome from the author, whose family did leave St. Louis for New York when she was young.

The moment: Minnelli began as an art director and designer, and his use of color is always fresh and fun -- there isn't another director in history who would have thought to put Judy Garland in purple gloves for the trolley ride, but once you see it, you can't imagine any other color.

In 1998, Scott Higgins wrote a thoughtful article for Style, "Color at the center: Minnelli's Technicolor style in 'Meet Me in St. Louis'" about the way Minnelli "uses color details continually to embellish compositions and generate striking harmonies." He points out that Minnelli's use of color in the film was contrary to the usual approach of the early Technicolor era to try to achieve a muted realism and that he also inverted the typical approach for musical numbers of putting the lead performer in the brightest color. (The best example of of that approach would come a few years later with Ann-Margret's unforgettable pink outfit and red hair in "Bye Bye Birdie's" "Got a Lot of Livin' To Do" dance number.) In the trolley scene, the surrounding characters are in an array of bright hues, but Garland is in black and white, with her only color the auburn hair and purple gloves, framing her perfectly.

I am very fond of gloves and this movie has some of my favorites. Other great movie gloves include "Woman of the Year" (Katherine Hepburn wears a wild pair with a matching and completely inappropriate outfit to her first baseball game), "Let's Make Love" (Marilyn Monroe wears exquisite white gloves for a meeting with the world's richest bachelor), "Gilda," (Rita Hayworth removes her gloves in the smoky "Put the Blame on Mame" dance number), "Breakfast at Tiffany's" (Audrey Hepburn is the essence of elegance in long, black gloves), and "The Age of Innocence" (Daniel Day Lewis unbuttons Michelle Pfeiffer's glove for a swooningly sensuous kiss on her wrist).

More musicals from Vincent Minnelli:

"Gigi"

"The Pirate"

"The Band Wagon"

"Bells Are Ringing"

§ § §

71

MEN IN BLACK
(1997)

Will Smith Passes the Test

The movie: "Men in Black" began as a 1990 comic book created and written by Lowell Cunningham. The men in black are part of a governmental organization that that monitors and suppresses paranormal activity on Earth, including extraterrestrials, demons, and mutants, keeping their activities secret to prevent mass hysteria. The film version from writer Ed Solomon ("Bill & Ted's Excellent Adventure") and director Barry Sonnenfeld ("Get Shorty," "The Addams Family"), has a tonal shift, playing the themes of paranoia and peril for humor rather than horror, and limiting the focus of the men in black to creatures from other planets, many benign but some bent on destroying our world. The comic book characters kill witnesses to keep word from getting out. The movie characters have a little pen-like instrument called a nebulizer that erases their memories.

This magnificently entertaining film is an excellent example of what a director's style can bring to a movie. As in "Get Shorty," Sonnenfeld creates a heightened and slightly skewed world, selling it through a clearly conceived tone and committed but understated performances from a cast of top professionals. Sonnenfeld has said that co-star Tommy Lee Jones told him he was not sure how to portray veteran MiB agent K ecause he was not experienced in comic roles. Sonnenfeld's wise advice was that K does not know he is in a comedy. And, of course, that is part of what makes him so funny. K's dry, deadpan delivery is just the counterpart to the wildness all around him from the aliens and the game but dumbfounded new recruit. One of the best line readings of the decade was when K is showing Edwards, who is about to become agent J (Will Smith) the alien technology the MiBs have collected, including a tiny new version of an audio CD. "Guess I'll have to buy *The White Album* again," he says as he goes on to the rest of the tour. Vincent D'Onofrio is marvelous as a bug-like alien who takes over the body of a surly farmer.

The moment: We first see police officer Edwards chasing after a perpetrator (stuntman and former national gymnastics champion Keith Campbell) in mid-town Manhattan. It seems to be a standard, if well-staged, action scene. But then the perp does a flip and starts climbing up the side of the Guggenheim Museum like an insect. Edwards chases him up to the roof, and when he gets close, he sees that the perp seems to have two sets of eyelids, one side-to-side. The perp says that the end of the world is coming and then jumps off the roof.

K questions Edwards about the perp's weapon and must be impressed with him because the next day, Edwards shows up for some sort of test. The other candidates are the "best of the best" from each branche of the military service. But they have no idea what they are being tested for. The first part is a written test with a number 2 pencil. It seems standard. But the test-takers have to sit in uncomfortable egg-shaped chairs and there is no hard surface to write on. The pencils break and pierce the test paper. All of the other candidates squirm around to try to make it work, but Edwards goes over to the coffee table and pulls it toward his chair with a loud screech, so he can use it to write on.

The next stage is a shooting gallery. The other candidates shoot the cardboard monsters and aliens, but Edwards hesitates and then shoots a cardboard little girl. When MiB agent Zed asks for an explanation, Edwards says,

> Well, first I was gonna pop this guy hanging from the street light, and I realized, y'know, he's just working out. I mean, how would I feel if somebody come runnin' in the gym and bust me in my ass while I'm on the treadmill? Then I saw this snarling beast guy, and I noticed he had a tissue in his hand, and I'm realizing, y'know, he's not snarling, he's sneezing. Y'know, ain't no real threat there. Then I saw little Tiffany. I'm thinking, y'know, eight-year-old white girl, middle of the ghetto, bunch of monsters, this time of night with quantum physics books? She about to start some shit, Zed. She's about eight years old, those books are WAY too advanced for her. If you ask me, I'd say she's up to something. And to be honest, I'd appreciate it if you eased up off my back about it.

Edwards passes by showing that his good instincts are not shaken by absurd, even shocking circumstances. And "the best of the best" get the nebulizer and go home.

More from Will Smith:

"Ali"

"Independence Day"

"The Pursuit of Happyness"

§ § §

72

Miss Firecracker
(1989)

Tango

The movie: There is quirky. And then there is Southern gothic. Playwright Beth Henley specializes in Southern grotesquery, and her plays "Crimes of the Heart" and "The Miss Firecracker Contest" have been made into movies with all-star casts, the actors clearly enjoying the chance to play outsize characters who act as though melodrama is, if not normal, at least natural. In "Crimes of the Heart," Oscar winners Diane Keaton, Jessica Lange, and Sissy Spacek play three sisters coping with a shriveled ovary, an inter-racial love affair with a teenage boy, and a husband-shooting followed by a refreshing glass of lemonade, all of this following the suicide of their mother when they were children. She killed the family cat before she died and the incomprehensibility of that act is as haunting as her abandonment of her daughters. When one of them says she realizes her mother wanted to take the cat with her because she did not want to be alone, for a moment the scope of the story becomes small and tender and compassionate.

In "Miss Firecracker," the main characters are Delmount (Tim Robbins), just out of a mental hospital and determined to sell the crumbling family mansion, his sister Elain (Mary Steenburgen), who was a legendary winner of the town's "Miss Firecracker" beauty pageant and has been asked to return for this year's contest to give a talk called, "My Life as a Beauty," and their cousin Carnelle (Holly Hunter), who desperately wants to win the title this time. Carnelle was orphaned at age 8 and came to live with her aunt and uncle and cousins. She never got over her feeling of abandonment and is embarrassed by the years she spent trying to compensate with attention-getting behavior that landed her the nickname of "Miss Hot Tamale." She thinks that if she can win the same title Elain did it will mean she has been accepted by the community and "leave in a blaze of glory."

But "Miss Firecracker" is supposed to have an unsullied reputation. Carnelle does not have Elain's conventional good looks, natural grace, or the self-absorption so often mistaken for poise. She does not have a gown to wear, so Carnelle asks Elain to bring the glamorous red dress she wore when she won and hopes it will make her a winner, too.

Director Thomas Schlamme ("Sports Night") has a gift for illuminating the humanity of characters who might otherwise come across as stylized or exaggerated. Perhaps the toughest challenge he faced here was a character named "Popeye," a black woman who sews fancy gowns for bullfrogs and has some dialog that borders on simple-minded. But with the brilliant actress Alfre Woodard, the character comes across as true-hearted and endearing. Steenburgen gives one of her best performances as Elain, whose superficial beauty queen charm barely conceals her spoiled and selfish spirit. Her "My Life as a Beauty" speech is one of the film's highlights. Scott Glen is also terrific as a rueful carny who genuinely cares for Carnelle.

The moment: There is a deliriously surreal brother-sister tango to "Cherry Pink and Apple Blossom White." With chaos all around them, Delmount and Elain dance slinkily through the house for a brief but delicious moment of affectionate understanding and shared memories. It could come across as random. But Schlamme, Robbins, and Steenburgen make it grounded, sincere, and golden.

More from Alfre Woodard:

    "Rich in Love"

    "Down in the Delta"

    "What's Cooking?"

    "Passion Fish"

    "Heart and Souls"

§ § §

73

Miss Tatlock's Millions (1948)

Ilka Chase Explains the Situation

The movie: "Miss Tatlock's Millions" is a nice little comedy that is almost never seen now because its premise is wildly inappropriate in today's more sensitive time. While that is legitimate, it is still worth watching, not because of its silly plotline or standard romance, but because it is a rare opportunity to see 1940's Broadway stars Dorothy Stickney and Ilka Chase.

These days, performers from film, reality television, and pop music are often used to add some luster to Broadway shows and some lucre to Broadway box offices. But the 1940's was still an era when there was more separation between movies and the more prestigious legitimate theater. So successful theatrical performers like Katherine Cornell, Helen Hayes, and Alfred Lunt and Lynn Fontanne, Laurette Taylor, and Ina Claire seldom appeared on screen and even though some of them were not comfortable performing in movies, it is still a lot of fun to watch them.

The story is about the heir to the title fortune, Schuyler Tatlock, a man we might describe today as developmentally disabled. He has been living in the tropics with a caretaker (Barry Fitzgerald as Noonan). Or so they thought. Noonan never told the Tatlock family that Schuyler disappeared. He has been living happily on his stipend, assuming they would never find out. When they tell him to bring Schuyler home, he needs someone to pretend to be the heir. He hires a Hollywood stunt man named Burke (John Lund), dies his hair, and tells him to act like -- well, you see how this could all seem insensitive. But Burke falls for Schuyler's sister Nan (a charming Wanda Hendrix), which foils the greedy relatives' plans to have her marry within the family connections (the prospective groom is a very young Robert Stack as Nickey van Alen).

The moment: When Nickey's mother (Ilka Chase) discovers that Burke is a fraud, she has a talk with him and explains that the best thing he can do for Nan is to go away and let her go on thinking he is Schuyler.

Chase is marvelous in this scene, resisting the temptation to overplay and make Mrs. van Alen a monster. She does not pretend to be outraged by someone who, after all, is doing what she is in trying to get some easy money.

She is also superb in "Now, Voyager" as the sympathetic sister-in-law of the repressed Charlotte Vale (Bette Davis).

Her first marriage was to actor Louis Calhern ("The Asphalt Jungle"). It lasted only seven months. When he married actress Julia Hoyt a few months later, Chase sent her the engraved "Mrs. Louis Calhern" stationery she had ordered for herself but not had time to use, with a note: "Dear Julia, I hope these reach you in time." It's worth making a special effort to see someone who could think that up.

One more note - the movie is directed by Richard Haydn, the British comic actor best known for providing the voice of the caterpillar in Disney's "Alice in Wonderland" and playing Max, the Von Trapp family's friend, in "The Sound of Music."

More glimpses of Broadway greats:

    Ina Claire in "Claudia" and "Ninotchka"

    Lunt and Fontanne in "The Guardsman"

Helen Hayes in "Airplane" and "What Every Woman Knows"

Margalo Gillmore in "The Happy Years" and "High Society"

Janice Paige in "Please Don't Eat the Daisies" and "Silk Stockings"

§ § §

74

Moving Midway
(2007)

The Nose, the Name, and the Plantation

The movie: "Moving Midway" is a superb documentary about the core elements of the American experience: family, identity, community, race, class, progress, the role of the past in directing the future, and real estate.

In declaring independence from England, one crucial element of the founding fathers' revolutionary ideas was the end of primogeniture, the law that passed all real property to the oldest male. This was an excellent system for stability and preservation of property, but as anyone who has ever read a Jane Austen book or watched "Downton Abbey" knows, it was disastrous to the financial security of the siblings of the oldest male.

After the American Revolution, the states abolished primogeniture in the spirit of freedom, equality, and opportunity. But in that same spirit, individuals were free to do as they liked with their property. The Hintons of North Carolina chose to leave the property they had owned since before the American Revolution to the oldest son of each generation so that, almost unique in this country, the land and its plantation building called Midway has been in the same family for more than 200 years. As we see from a portrait of an ancestor that still hangs in the house, the family nose has passed down to many of the descendents as well.

As the movie opens, New York film critic Godfrey Cheshire learns that his cousin Charlie Hinton Silver, the current owner of Midway, wants to move the building to another part of the property. Ownership of Midway may have stayed the same for two centuries, but the world around it has changed and a shopping mall and busy streets are too near the house. Some family members are concerned, especially one aunt who worries that the family ghost will not be happy with the move. This is the first of several layers in the film about reconciling change and tradition.

The next layer comes about when Cheshire meets for the first time Robert Hinton, Associate Director of Africana Studies at New York University. Hinton is part of an extended black family descended from the slaves held by the Hinton family, and, apparently, descended from the white Hintons as well. Unlike Cheshire and Silver, Professor Hinton has the family surname. He also has the family nose. The white Hinton family, very steeped in their history over the past two centuries, has to revise what they thought they knew as they meet members of their family they had never imagined. Professor Hinton joined the film as chief historian and associate producer.

He brought some of his family to the story, including Abraham Lincoln Hinton, born in 1909, who says his father, born in 1848, told him that Midway was his birthplace.

The two branches of the family have very different views about Midway, a name that grows in resonance through the course of the film. One black Hinton says he is glad the property will be covered with cement so that nothing can grow where his slave ancestors planted crops. A white Hinton says hopefully that she is sure her ancestors treated their slaves well because her family is all so nice they must have been descended from nice people. Robert Hinton, who at one point acknowledges that in New York he feels more kinship with white Southerners than with urban blacks, makes a comment that summarizes the film's rueful but hopeful theme: "I always wanted to meet a white Hinton. I was hoping I would hate him. The problem is, I like you, so I can't lay a lot of stuff on you."

The moment: When Robert Hinton first arrives at Midway, he is told, a bit sheepishly, that one relative is not there because he is participating in a Civil War re-enactment and asked if that offends him. His response is perfect: "I'm comfortable with the idea that they keep refighting it, as long as they keep losing it."

More documentaries about the American South:

"Sherman's March"

"Dear Jesse"

"Searching for the Wrong-Eyed Jesus"

§ § §

75

MR. BLANDINGS BUILDS HIS DREAM HOUSE (1948)

Myrna Loy Talks to the Painters

The movie: Eric Hodgins was editor and later publisher of Fortune Magazine, but he is best remembered today for his novel based on his experience in renovating a home in Connecticut, *Mr. Blandings Builds His Dream House*, published in 1946 and made into a film with Cary Grant and Myrna Loy two years later.

Blandings is an advertising executive with a wife and two daughters who live in a small Manhattan apartment. They decide to move to Connecticut and find what seems to be a perfect old farmhouse. But it is structurally unsound and has to be torn down. This gives them the opportunity to fantasize about their dream house, so they make a list of everything they can think of, only to discover that it would be several times their budget. They decide on something more affordable and then the misery begins for them and the fun begins for the audience, as they are subjected to every possible indignity, muddle, and cost escalation anyone who has ever hired a contractor will appreciate. The screenplay, adapted by the always-reliable Norman Panama and Melvin Frank ("The Court Jester," "White Christmas") wisely makes the hapless couple rather than the workmen the target of most of the humor. And Grant and Loy are at their best, which means as good as it gets.

Some elements of the film do not hold up well, especially a subplot that has Blandings getting jealous of his best friend's relationship with Mrs. B. The portrayal of Gussie (Louise Beavers), the Blandings maid, is, if not racist, insensitive by today's standards. It is worth taking a moment to consider her role in the story.

Blandings works in advertising, an emerging field that was the subject of some barbed satire in this era in films like "It's Always Fair Weather," "Will Success Spoil Rock Hunter?" and "The Hucksters." One of his daughters tells Blandings what her teacher has to say about his profession: "Miss Stellwagon says advertising makes people who can't afford it buy things they don't want, with money they haven't got."

Throughout the film, one of Blandings' biggest problems is finding a new slogan for a ham made by his client, Wham. The eureka moment comes when Gussie says, "If you ain't eating Wham, you ain't eating ham!" "Darling, give Gussie a ten dollar raise!" says Mr. Blandings. The happy ending includes Gussie's smiling face in an ad featuring her slogan. As often happens in movies of this era, an African-American character serves as truth-teller whose idea is unquestioningly appropriated by the movie's hero. It would be nice to think that Gussie's suggestion today would lead not to a ten-dollar raise but to a job at the advertising agency.

The moment: One of the highlights of "Mr. Blandings Builds His Dream House" is Mrs. Blandings' instructions to the painters and their response, perfectly encapsulating the chasm between the aspirations of the homeowner and the realities of renovations.

> *Muriel Blandings: I want it to be a soft green, not as blue-green as a robin's egg, but not as yellow-green as daffodil buds. Now, the only sample I could get is a little too yellow, but don't let whoever does it go to the other extreme and get it too blue. It should just be a sort of grayish-yellow-green. Now, the dining room. I'd like yellow. Not just yellow; a very gay yellow. Something*

bright and sunshine-y. I tell you, Mr. PeDelford, if you'll send one of your men to the grocer for a pound of their best butter, and match that exactly, you can't go wrong! Now, this is the paper we're going to use in the hall. It's flowered, but I don't want the ceiling to match any of the colors of the flowers. There's some little dots in the background, and it's these dots I want you to match. Not the little greenish dot near the hollyhock leaf, but the little bluish dot between the rosebud and the delphinium blossom. Is that clear? Now the kitchen is to be white. Not a cold, antiseptic hospital white. A little warmer, but still, not to suggest any other color but white. Now for the powder room -- in here -- I want you to match this thread, and don't lose it. It's the only spool I have and I had an awful time finding it! As you can see, it's practically an apple red. Somewhere between a healthy winesap and an unripened Jonathan. Oh, excuse me...

Mr. PeDelford: You got that Charlie?

Charlie, Painter: Red, green, blue, yellow, white.

Mr. PeDelford: Check.

More movies about home renovations:

"George Washington Slept Here"

"The Money Pit"

§ § §

76

NATIONAL VELVET (1944)

A Breathtaking Piece of Folly

The movie: "National Velvet" one of the greatest family films ever made, taps into one of the oldest, deepest dreams, the dream of horses. Every child dreams of controlling these huge, powerful, loyal creatures, of flying over hurdles on their backs, of earning their devotion and of being devoted to them in return. And then there is the dream of racing, as Velvet (Elizabeth Taylor) says in this movie, "until you burst your heart, and then until you burst it again, and then until you burst it twice as much as before," until the two of you explode past the finish line ahead of everyone else.

A very young Taylor and Mickey Rooney are superb as Velvet, a sheltered girl from a strict but loving family, and Mi, the rough boy who has seen a lot of hardship. She knows about horses because she loves them. He knows about racing because he has seen it. Velvet's faith in both Mi and the Pi is at the center of the movie. She accepts them both immediately and irrevocably, though both are mistrusted by others. She does not believe Mi when he says he doesn't like horses, and when he says he is only interested in the race for the money. She knows that he feels as passionately about the Pi as she does, though he cannot say it, or even admit it to himself.

This is the story of dreams themselves, wise and foolish, big and small, realized and impossible, and about the way all of these dreams change those who are lucky enough to dream them. It is about the importance of faith -- Velvet's faith in herself and in the horse she names Pi and in her dream, and her family's faith in her and in Mi -- and the importance of that belief and support in making the dream come true. Mi says, "You bit off a big piece of dream for yourself, Velvet." But her dream is not for fame or fortune. She wants her horse to enter the biggest race in England so that he will have a chance to be truly great. She knows that by riding him herself she will disqualify him because girls are not allowed to ride in the Grand National race. But she knows if she rides him, they will both win in the ways that really matter.

But most of all, "National Velvet" is the story of a loving family. It is very different in many ways from the families that the American children of today know -- for example, the mother and father (Oscar-winner Anne Revere and Donald Crisp) are so reserved that they call each other "Mr. and Mrs. Brown" until the very last scene. But their affection for each other is always evident.

Before she was blacklisted during the Red Scare, Revere played three of the most iconic mothers ever put on screen. She was John Garfield's tough mother in the boxing classic, "Body and Soul." And in the Best Picture Oscar winner "Gentlemen's Agreement," she has a wonderful scene with Gregory Peck as her reporter son, telling him how proud she is of his pioneering exposé of anti-Semitism. She says,

> *You know something, Phil? I suddenly want to live to be very old. Very. I want to be around to see what happens. The world is stirring in very strange ways. Maybe this is the century for it. Maybe that's why it's so troubled. Other centuries had their driving forces. What will ours have been when men look back? Maybe it won't be the American century after all... or the Russian century or the atomic century. Wouldn't it be wonderful... if it turned out to be everybody's century... when people all over the world -- free people -- found a way to live together? I'd like to be around to see some of that... even the begin-*

ning. I may stick around for quite a while.

The moment: In one of the sweetest scenes ever filmed, Mrs. Brown takes out the 100 gold pieces she won as a young woman for swimming the Channel, and gives them to Velvet. There were a thousand times the family could have used that money, but she was saving it for a dream as big as her own once was. This most practical of women understands her daughter and tells Velvet, "I too believe that everyone should have a chance at a breathtaking piece of folly once in his life." As they leave for the race, Velvet says to Mrs. Brown, "You'll be proud of the Pi, mother." Mrs. Brown says, "I want to be proud of you." And she is.

More great movie mothers:

"Dumbo"

"Little Women"

"I Remember Mama"

"Sounder"

"Cheaper by the Dozen" (1950)

"What's Cooking?"

§ § §

77

Notorious
(1946)

The Kiss

The movie: "Notorious" was reputed to be Alfred Hitchcock's own favorite of all his movies, and it was the acknowledged favorite of critic-turned filmmaker Francois Truffaut, whose book-length interview of Hitchcock is essential reading for anyone who wants to understand the way movies tell stories. Hitchcock biographer Donald Spoto wrote, "'Notorious' is in fact Alfred Hitchcock's first attempt--at the age of forty-six--to bring his talents to the creation of a serious love story, and its story of two men in love with Ingrid Bergman could only have been made at this stage of his life."

Bergman plays Alicia Huberman, the daughter of a Nazi spy. Humiliated by his trial and conviction and the assumption of everyone she knows that she was helping her father, she has tried to lose herself in wild parties and bad behavior. But T.R. Devlin (Cary Grant), an American agent who has overheard the wiretaps of Alicia's conversations with her father, knows that she is loyal to the United States. He persuades her to go to work for the American government as a spy, using her father's connections. One of his old associates, Alexander Sebastian (Claude Rains) is living in Brazil with some other Nazi refugees. Devlin takes Alicia there to meet up with Sebastian and find out what he is hiding. In order to infiltrate thoroughly enough to find out, Alicia has to accept Sebastian's marriage proposal and move into his home. Under the watchful eye of Sebastian's suspicious mother, Alicia must, like Bluebeard's wife, steal the key to unlock the door and uncover what has been hidden.

This is a gripping story and the scene where Alicia hides the key is a small masterpiece of tension and suspense. The overlay of the complicated relationship between Devlin and Alicia adds enormous dramatic power to the storyline. Both use a tough exterior to hide their feelings. The suspense of the emotional connection between them is even more compelling than the spy story. Will Devlin refuse to acknowledge his feelings for Alicia because of his professional obligations or because he cannot bear to admit to himself the risks he has urged her to accept? Will he be so blinded by that refusal that he will put her at even greater risk?

The moment: And that is what makes their kiss so meaningful.

These days, most romantic movies are dreadful because the script cannot think of a good reason to keep them from going to bed together in the first 20 minutes of the story. (*Twilight* author Stephanie Meyer has acknowledged that the reason she made her main character a vampire was to provide a meaningful -- if fantasy -- obstacle to physical contact.) In "Notorious," there are story and psychological barriers keeping them apart. Even worse, Alicia is (presumably) having sex with someone else as a part of her cover. And yet, the longing they have for each other is evident and by the time it finally happens, we are almost as anxious for them to have some overt confession of their true feelings as they are.

And then, at long, long last, they kiss. And in an art form that has spent more time than any other on the kiss, this one just might be the very best in the history of the movies. The Hays Production Code banned kisses of longer than three seconds. So, Hitchcock told Bergman and Grant to just keep kissing, stopping to murmur to each other and nuzzle, and then kiss again. They move from the balcony overlooking the ocean into the room, talking about dinner and calling the hotel as though they are talking about sex, and as though being more than two inches apart is unbearable. "This is a very strange love affair," Alicia almost whispers as he is calling his hotel to ask for his messages, still embracing. "Why?" Devlin asks. "Maybe the fact that you don't love me." "When I don't love you, I'll let you know." It is a scene of piercing intimacy.

Another great movie kissing scene also involves a telephone call. In "It's a Wonderful Life," George Bailey (James Stewart) is sharing the phone with Mary Hatch (Donna Reed), doing his best not to fall in love with her and refusing to admit that he already has. They listen to their friend go on about his business opportunity as George fights his emotions. Finally, the very closeness of Mary is just too much and he just grabs her.

More with Ingrid Bergman:

"Casablanca"

"Gaslight"

"Cactus Flower"

"Spellbound"

§ § §

78

Postcards from the Edge (1990)

Making Up

The movie: Before Carrie Fisher told her wildly dysfunctional and multiply married family's story more directly with her book and one-woman show, "Wishful Drinking," she wrote a fictionalized version, first a novel and then a movie called "Postcards from the Edge." Meryl Streep plays Suzanne, a young actress with a substance abuse problem and a tendency to hide her vulnerability with brittle epigrams and smart-alecky comments like "Instant gratification takes too long."

Fisher is the daughter of Debbie Reynolds and Eddie Fisher. Her fictional stand-in is Suzanne, the daughter of a one-time movie star named Doris Mann (Shirley MacLaine). She resents her mother's flamboyant self-absorption, the way she sucks all the oxygen out of a room. But she also loves and admires her mother's indomitable spirit even as she worries that her mother's example demonstrates that survival requires more resilience than she can muster.

At a party Doris gives for Suzanne's return from rehab, Doris coaxes Suzanne to sing and the song she picks is telling: "You Don't Know Me." But Doris is at heart a performer first, and so when Suzanne is done, she gets up to belt out a cabaret version of Stephen Sondheim's "I'm Still Here." She does not mean to be competitive. She has just been a star so long she does not know how to be anything else.

The moment: Near the end of the film, Doris drives while tipsy and hits a tree. Suzanne goes to get her at the hospital, where Doris is shaken but not badly hurt.

Both of them are so used to living publicly that it seems perfectly natural that Doris' primary concern is the paparazzi she knows will be waiting outside. She got blood on her wig so had to take it off. As she explained earlier, her eyebrows were shaved for a movie when she was a young actress and they never grew back. With her wisps of hair and scrubbed face, she looks old and fragile and nothing like a movie star.

Tenderly, Suzanne takes out Doris' makeup and starts fixing her face, tying a stylish scarf over her head to add some glamour. The daughter cares for her mother in a way that communicates everything she could not find the words to say.

More makeup moments:

"Super 8" A teenager working on a movie project with his friends finds himself in an unexpected and unsettling but not unpleasantly intimate moment as he applies zombie make-up to the face of the girl he likes.

"Dangerous Liaisons" The manipulative Marquise Isabelle de Merteuil realizes that the social position and power she cares about deeply has been destroyed and she removes her makeup, staring dully at her reflection.

"Brick" Meagan Good wears Kabuki makeup in a scene from this strikingly stylized mystery film set in a high school.

§ § §

79

THE POSTMAN ALWAYS RINGS TWICE (1946)

Lana's Entrance

The movie: One of the most electrifying images ever put on film is Lana Turner's entrance in the steamy film noir classic "The Postman Always Rings Twice."

James M. Cain was a journalist who turned to fiction. He was a master of dark, twisted, pulpy, stories about lust and envy and greed and betrayal. His characters claw their way to top no matter what it takes. They lie, steal, and kill. Two more iconic films of the 1940's are based on Cain's books, "Mildred Pierce" (recently remade as a miniseries with Kate Winslet) and "Double Indemnity."

No actor ever showed more soul on screen than John Garfield. He made such a powerful impression in his first role, a movie called "Four Daughters," that he was nominated for an Oscar. And his character was brought back for the sequel even though he was supposed to have been killed in the first one. If he had not died so young, only 39 years old, he would be remembered along with Humphrey Bogart and James Cagney.

Even when Garfield's characters do bad things, we can see it comes from a place of anguish, not evil. Here he plays Frank, a drifter dropped off near a small diner and gas station next to a highway. The owner, Nick (pixyish Cecil Kellaway), offers him a job with room and board. Frank says he has a problem with settling down. "My feet. They keep itching me to go places." Nick persuades Frank to come inside the diner for a burger, puts the meat on the grill, and then has to run out for a customer who needs gas.

The moment: And then Frank looks over to the doorway. We see her feet first in her white shoes, and then her lovely, bare legs, tiny white shorts and midriff-baring top, and the white turban tied around her hair. It is Lana Turner as Cora, and she is dazzling.

The movie is in black and white but up to this point it

has all been shades of gray. Cinematographer Sidney Wagner films Cora's clothes in this first scene and throughout the film in the glowing white of detergent commercials. Her blonde, blonde hair and pale skin are warm and luminous in the dusty surroundings. For a brief moment before her looks coarsened, Turner was the most beautiful creature on earth and all of us are lucky that the moment was put on film so we can all sigh along with Frank, more than seventy years later.

Cora has dropped her lipstick (in a white case). It rolls across the floor over to Frank. She reaches out her hand for it without moving forward. He makes her walk over to him to get it back. By the time he puts it in her hand, we can tell that they will do terrible things for and then to each other. And we know that Frank knows that, too, and we can understand why he knows it will be worth it.

More of Lana Turner at her peak:

"Ziegfeld Girl"

"Love Finds Andy Hardy"

More of John Garfield:

"Body and Soul"

"Gentlemen's Agreement"

§ § §

80

Pulp Fiction
(1994)

The Briefcase MacGuffin

The movie: The broom of the Wicked Witch of the West. The Maltese Falcon. The intercostal clavicle. The Lost Ark of the Covenant. The Holy Grail. Unobtanium. The secret formula. The hidden treasure. The kidnapped girl. The serial killer. These are all examples of what Alfred Hitchcock dubbed "the MacGuffin" - shorthand for whatever it is that the hero and heroine are after. It has to be described so economically that it does not distract us from the real story, which is the chase. But it has to be described so compellingly that we are invested in the hero's efforts to obtain it.

"Pulp Fiction" is a twisted, brutal, wildly quotable and narratively innovative film with intersecting stories that connect several groups of big and small-time criminals. Co-writer/director Quentin Tarantino maintains an arch, highly stylized tone that puts a knowing, ironic gloss on the intense violence and sordid encounters. He does this through his masterful control of the movie's visuals, the placement and movement of the camera and the production design, through a brilliantly selected score of what he dubbed "surfer spaghetti western" songs, and through his inimitable dialog, brash, profane, philosophical, and drenched in pop culture.

One of the intersecting storylines involves a tough gangster named Marcellus Wallace (Ving Rhames), who sends two of his hit men (played by John Travolta and Samuel L. Jackson) to retrieve a briefcase that has been stolen from him from some foolish and hopelessly overmatched young men who look like college kids.

The moment: The hit men open the briefcase.

Tarantino originally intended to put diamonds in the briefcase but rejected it as too mundane. Instead, he never lets the audience see what is inside. All we know is that it glows (an orange light bulb was placed inside for filming) and that it has a mesmerizing effect on those who look at it.

The mysterious briefcase has led to speculation at all levels, from Internet discussion boards to scholarly analyses. Some see this as another of the many references to other films in "Pulp Fiction." In "Kiss Me Deadly," there is a briefcase with glowing contents (radioactive material). A very popular theory suggests that it is Marcellus' soul. The basis for this claim includes the case's combination lock code: it is 666, the "Number of the Beast" according to the Book of Revelation. And Marcellus has a band-aid on the back of his neck, the place from which souls are said to be extracted.

Tarantino insists that he specifically intended not to have any explanation for the contents of the briefcase, though he played with speculators in a filmed interview with his friend and "Grindhouse" co-director, Robert Rodriguez. Just as he appeared about to reveal the truth about the briefcase, there is a "missing reel" title card. And then the interview resumes and Rodriguez, apparently enlightened, says that this new knowledge has radically changed his appreciation for the film. But of course it is leaving it open to interpretation that makes the briefcase an ideal MacGuffin.

Jackson said in a 1995 Playboy interview that Tarantino told him what was inside the briefcase was "Whatever you want it to be."

> So I assumed it was something that, when people looked at it, seemed like the most beautiful thing they had ever seen or their greatest desire. When I looked inside, be-

tween scenes, I saw two lights and some batteries. What I would have wanted to see are the next ten films I'm going to do and hope they're all as good as "Pulp Fiction."

More classic MacGuffins:

"The Maltese Falcon"

"Raiders of the Lost Ark"

"Bringing Up Baby"

§ § §

81

RAIDERS OF THE LOST ARK
(1981)

I Know a Villain Who Swallowed a Fly

The movie: The two biggest box-office giants in history combined forces for a film that set a new standard for adventure on screen. Steven Spielberg and George Lucas gave us the two-fisted professor of archeology, Indiana Jones (Harrison Ford), on a mission to find the greatest lost artifact of all time, the lost Ark of the Covenant containing the original tablets with the Ten Commandments.

Spielberg and Lucas are justifiably famous for their meticulous attention to detail and every sequence was carefully mapped out in advance. But some of the movie's best moments were unplanned and it is a tribute to the filmmakers that they remained open to the possibilities that occurred while filming. One of the best-loved sequences in the movie has an enormous, menacing black-clad swordsman brandishing his scimitar. The original script had an elaborate swordfight sketched out over three pages and was scheduled to take three days to shoot. But Ford was ill and exhausted and suggested he just pull out his gun and shoot the guy. It worked so well they did a funny variation on that moment in the sequel.

The moment: They filmed in Tunisia, where temperatures rose to 130 degrees. Everyone had to hold their hands in front of their mouths to keep out the flies looking for shade. Paul Freeman, playing Nazi-funded villain Dr. René

Belloq, was saying his line about Jones giving mercenaries a bad name when a fly crawled into his mouth on camera. He just swallowed it and kept going. That is, as actors say, how to commit. It is nothing that anyone would have scripted but it works well to show the character's ruthless single-mindedness. It makes him literally bloodthirsty.

More bad guys with animals:

"You Only Live Twice" (Blofeld's cat)

The "Austin Powers" series (Dr. Evil's hairless cat)

"The Little Mermaid" (Ursula's eels)

§ § §

82

RICH IN LOVE
(1992)

"I've Been Loving You Too Long"

The movie: "Rich in Love" is not a great film but I am enormously fond of it. For one thing, of all the beautiful homes in all the movies I have ever seen, this is the house I would most like to own. It is not especially striking in design or elegant. It just has a nice, comfortable, lived-in feeling and a magnificent location right on the water in Charleston, South Carolina.

And I like the characters in the movie. They also have a comfortable, lived-in feeling, even though some of them are going through a very stressful period. The screenwriter (Alfred Uhry) and director (Bruce Beresford) of "Driving Miss Daisy" reunited for another Southern tale and its sense of place is like another character in the story.

It is told from the point of view of an ultra-responsible high school senior named Lucille Odem (Kathryn Erbe of "Law & Order: Criminal Intent"). As it opens, she comes home to find that her mother has left home, leaving a note. Lucille's father (Albert Finney) is about to arrive. Lucille can't get her mother back before he finds out, so all she can do is rewrite the note to make its tone gentler and more rueful. She is trying to protect his feelings but this only makes her mother's departure even more inexplicable and gives her father false hope.

As days go by without any further message from Mrs. Odem, Lucille tries to help her father find a way to adjust while they struggle to understand what has happened. And then Lucille's careless and self-involved older sister Rae (Suzy Amis of "Titanic") shows up unexpectedly with a couple of surprises. She has brought along a man named Billy (Kyle MacLachlan). She is pregnant and she and Billy are married.

The moment: They go to a small local nightclub, where Rae is greeted warmly by the owner, who asks her to sing. She gets up and (with the help of the voice of singer Suzie Benson) delivers a knockout performance of "I've Been Loving You Too Long to Stop Now."

It's a knockout in more ways than one. While it plays a role in bringing the plot and understanding of the characters forward (especially in showing us that Billy does not know his new wife very well), it is such a stunning moment that it knocks the film off its wheels a bit. But I couldn't bear to think of editing it out; it is magnificent.

One more great moment in the film is in a scene with the wonderful Alfre Woodard as Rhody, who plays Mrs. Odem's friend and confidante. When Lucille, still trying to make everything work out in the way she thinks will make everyone happy, tells Rhody she just wants everything to get back to normal, Rhody says kindly, "That's the problem with normal; it keeps changing on you."

More from Albert Finney:

"Erin Brockovich"

"Tom Jones"

"Two for the Road"

"Shoot the Moon"

83

Rudy
(1993)

The Score

The movie: Daniel "Rudy" Ruettiger had a dream. He wanted to play football for Notre Dame. He did not have the money, the grades, or the athletic ability, and he was too small. But he had the determination. And he did it.

And then he had another dream. He wanted his story to be a movie. And he achieved that dream, too. He was played by Sean Astin in one of the most heartwarming sports films of the decade.

"Rudy" is everything a sports movie should be. It has an underdog. It has setbacks. It has long, hard, tough road to get to where he wants to be. And it is true. Rudy's goal is audacious, even impossible in some ways. But in another way it is endearingly modest. He does not hope to win the big game or even make a touchdown or catch a pass. He just wants to be a part of the team. And if the best way for him to help the team is to be a human tackle dummy during practices, he will do that gladly and give it everything he has every time.

It will make you cry. Some people can hold out to the end but I start to lose it when Rudy asks the new coach to keep the previous coach's promise to let him out onto the field in a game so his name will be on the official record. The coach turns him down and then one after the other, the players come in and place their enormous jerseys on the coach's desk. If Rudy cannot play, they will not play either. It is the coach who gets a lesson in what it is to be a team.

Like "Hoosiers," also directed by David Anspaugh and written by Angelo Pizzo, "Rudy" has a burnished, Midwestern glow and there is a quiet, spacious, almost cathedral-like feel to the place where the game is played.

The moment: "Are you ready?" the coach asks Rudy in the last ten seconds of the last game before he graduates, to go out on the field for the first time. "I've been ready my whole life," he says.

The crowd is chanting, "Rudy! Rudy!" Rudy's father and brother and best friend (Jon Favreau in his movie debut) are in the stands, overjoyed. (The real Rudy is in the stands, too.) So there is just one more thing we need to achieve the ultimate movie moment and this is where "Rudy" really delivers: the stirring score by Jerry Goldsmith. Credited as composer on 251 films, Goldsmith worked on dramas, comedies, thrillers, sci-fi, historical films, and television shows. He wrote music for "Rio Lobo," "Poltergeist," "Patton," "Seven Days in May," the first "Star Trek" movie, and "Escape from the Planet of the Apes." He was nominated for Oscars 17 times and won for "The Omen." But this is my favorite of his movie scores because it so perfectly fits the moment. As Rudy goes out onto the field his theme, simple and a little bittersweet then builds to a full orchestral triumph. There is no better example of music telling the story than this one.

A very different but equally effective use of music is in the final scene of "The King's Speech." They originally used Beethoven's Seventh Symphony as a temporary track, expecting composer Alexander Desplat, who provided a fine score for the film, to write something to replace it. Hooper told me it was Desplat's idea to keep the Beethoven. He quoted Desplat: "The reason that choice is so good is that Beethoven exists in our public imagination, our public space. It helps to elevate the speech to the status of a public event instead of a private event. No film score can do that because it's always internal to the movie." Desplat is one of the best composers working in films today, and this story shows that, like all great creators of movie scores, his commitment is to what works for the movie.

In "Rudy," Goldsmith's original score perfectly compliments Rudy's struggle, his dream, his passion, and his moment on the field, for the record books.

More magnificent movie scores:

"The Godfather"

"The Magnificent Seven"

"The Adventures of Robin Hood"

"To Kill a Mockingbird"

"Picnic"

"Two for the Road"

§ § §

84

School Daze
(1988)

Who are the Wannabees?

The movie: Writer-director Spike Lee's films get a lot of attention for being provocative, even confrontational. Films like "Do the Right Thing," "She's Gotta Have It," "Jungle Fever," "Malcolm X," and "Bamboozled" are sometimes debated as though they were not stories but op-eds or political arguments. In a sense they are; Lee is fearless about engaging on and off-screen in a conversation about race and equality. His documentary films about Hurricane Katrina, "If God is Willing and da Creek Don't Rise" and "When the Levees Broke" are stunning, disturbing, and filled with justifiable outrage. People sometimes overlook how talented he is as a director. "Inside Man" is a brilliant heist film and a masterwork of cinematic storytelling.

I am a huge fan of Lee's work and I have particular affection for his second film, "School Daze," inspired in part by his own experiences at Morehouse College. The focus is on the battles between two groups on campus. One active and outspoken group led by Dap (Laurence Fishburne) is very politically engaged. As with many schools at the time, they are pushing the college's endowment to divest stock holdings in companies that were doing business with the racist Apartheid regime in South Africa. They think they have a claim on authenticity because of their awareness of their African heritage and their commitment to equality and social justice. The young women keep their hair natural.

The other group cares about sororities and fraternities and fitting in rather than challenging the establishment. The young women process their hair and look down on their darker skinned classmates.

And they like parties. This was the movie that introduced audiences to a bathing suit party where everyone danced to a song called "Da Butt."

Some people are put off by the movie's inconsistent tone and narrative messiness. Unlike most American films, every plot line does not get tied up neatly. That is consistent with the film's themes of identity and authenticity. It makes sense that a movie about finding who you are would teeter between comedy and drama, gritty realism and a heightened reality. With musical numbers.

This is an extraordinary achievement filled with memorable moments. Some of the highlights include the step dance-off and the singing battle between the "Wannabees" (as in "Wanna be better than you" or "Wanna be white") and the "Jigaboos" (the lighter-skinned African American students appropriate the racist epithet used by bigoted whites about all black people). Dap has looked down on his cousin (played by Lee himself) for wanting to be a part of the fraternity system. But when it comes to the step competition, both sides compete the same way.

The moment: The battle between the two on-campus groups is completely reframed, though, in one of the most powerful scenes of the last 25 years, when Dap and his friends decide to go off campus for some fast food. The young men who are so sure that they represent the authentic African-American experience because of their true hearts and good intentions find that the local African-American men do not see them as the promise of the future but as betrayers of the past. To these men, Dap and his friends are just another kind of "Wannabee." The gulf between them is heart-wrenching, poignant, and compelling.

Some also objected, to the movie's unusual last scene, with Dap yelling to the camera in a tight close-up, "WAKE UP!" But almost 25 years later, it is still a message everyone needs to hear.

More Spike Lee:

"She's Gotta Have It"

"Malcolm X"

"Bamboozled"

"Do the Right Thing"

"Inside Man"

"The 25th Hour"

"When the Levees Broke"

§ § §

85

The Shining
(1980)

Jack's Book

The movie: Writer-director Stanley Kubrick took Stephen King's novel about a boy with psychic powers and made it into his own meditation on what really, really scares us. I am by no means an expert on scary movies, but I do know that fear is as highly personal as comedy. As George Orwell demonstrated so unforgettably in 1984, each of us has our own idea of what terrifies us most. This one is at the top of my list for the scariest scene ever, and I am not referring to the tsunami of blood gushing out of the elevator or the chase scene with the ax or even the insanely creepy photograph at the end. The scariest moment I've ever seen in a movie is when Shelley Duvall finds out what is in Jack Nicholson's typewriter.

Duvall plays Wendy Torrence, a young wife and mother who goes with her husband, Jack (Jack Nicholson) and their son Danny (Danny Lloyd) to be winter caretakers at an enormous hotel. They will be snowed in and isolated there for months. Jack hopes to use the time to work on his novel. Wendy hopes that it will provide them with some peace and quiet. Jack has had a drinking problem and once hurt Danny when he was drunk. Wendy does not know that Danny has the power of telepathy and precognition ("shining").

Danny has a premonition before they go to the hotel that makes him think there is something wrong, especially in room 237. At first, Danny and his mother enjoy exploring the hotel. Danny rides his hot wheels through the long hallways and they try out the maze outdoors. But then Jack begins to be moody and strange, and Wendy gets worried.

The moment: Wendy is reassured when she hears Jack typing away until, in a scene added by Kubrick, she takes a look at what he has been writing.

It is just the same sentence, over and over again, single-spaced and double-spaced, on hundreds of pages: "All work and no play makes Jack a dull boy." The chilling evidence of Jack's deranged compulsions and the danger it poses for Wendy and Danny is devastating.

Kubrick shot different takes of Wendy reading the typewriter pages in different languages for the international release of the film. He found an equivalent proverb for each language.

"The Shining" was re-made for television seventeen years later. It was truer to King's book but Kubrick's version is an undisputed masterpiece, enormously influential and endlessly studied, copied, referred to, and parodied. Most recently, it was the subject of a documentary called "Room

237" about the intense focus and theorizing by fans of the film. And it reveals a detail most viewers will not notice, at least not consciously. Kubrick used different typewriters in the various shots of Jack at work, contributing to the sense of disorientation and unease for the audience.

More Stephen King movies:

"Carrie"

"Stand By Me"

"The Shawshank Redemption"

"Sleepwalkers"

"The Green Mile"

"Misery"

§ § §

86

Sounder
(1972)

John A. Alonzo Shows Us the Beauty of Black Skin

The movie: "Sounder" is based on the Newberry Award-winning book by William H. Armstrong about the struggles of a black sharecropper family the father is sent to prison for stealing a ham to feed his family. Screenwriter Lonne Elder III became the first African-American to be nominated for a Best Screenplay Oscar.

Sounder is the family dog (and the only character in the book with a name). While the father (Paul Winfield) is gone, the mother (Cecily Tyson) tries to find out where he has been sent (local rules prohibit release of that information about black prisoners) and sends her oldest son, David (Kevin Hooks) to try to find him. He fails, but on his travels he meets a teacher who offers him the opportunity to live with her so he can get an education. The screenplay softens some of the bleakness of the novel but both center on the boy's yearning for an education even as he worries about leaving his family. In 2002, ABC's "Wonderful World of Disney" had a remake of this film, reuniting two of the original cast. Hooks directed, and Winfield appeared as the clergyman.

Director Martin Ritt was a New Yorker who went to college in North Carolina and he had a special gift for evoking the rhythms, cadences, atmosphere, sounds, and textures of the American South, as he showed in films like "The Long Hot Summer" and "Norma Rae." He understands the eloquence of silence, and its power. This is an enormously moving film.

The moment: Black performers in movies are often inadequately lit and photographed, especially if there are white actors in the same shot. Cinematographer John A. Alonzo was one of the first and still one of the best to show the beautiful golden undertones of African-American skin. He lights each actor's face to make sure we get to see every nuance of their sensitive performances. This movie's "moment" is just the pleasure of seeing the sunlight of the Deep South illuminate these extraordinary actors.

More cinematographers who showed special skill in photographing actors of color:

Frederick Elmes in "The Namesake"

Ernest R. Dickerson in "Do the Right Thing"

Matthew Libatique in "Inside Man"

Roberto Schaefer in "Monster's Ball"

§ § §

87

STATE FAIR
(1945)

Judging the Mincemeat Competition

The movie: Richard Rodgers and Oscar Hammerstein created the modern Broadway musical with "Oklahoma" in 1943. It integrated the songs and story and had a natural, American setting. Their other plays continued to push boundaries with ambitious and serious themes. They confronted racial prejudice and often included tragic deaths of important characters. But in their only score written directly for the movies, they chose a lighter subject, a remake of a 1933 non-musical film starring Will Rogers about an Iowa farm family attending the state fair, with a disappointing remake in 1962 starring Pat Boone and Ann-Margret. They also chose a less serious subject for their one score written directly for television, "Cinderella," originally starring Lesley Ann Warren and then remade with Brandy and Whitney Houston.

The story of "State Fair" is very simple. Everyone in the Frake family is excited about the fair, one of the most exciting events of the year. Margy's father (Charles Winninger) has a hog and her mother (Fay Bainter) has her mincemeat and both are hoping for blue ribbons in competition. In keeping with the classic themes of movie journeys, everyone will go to the fair looking for something and everyone will come home changed by the experience.

Rodgers and Hammerstein won their only Oscar for "State Fair's" "It Might as Well Be Spring," sung by the farmer's daughter Margy Frake (Jeanne Crain) at the beginning of the film. The lyrics say it may be the end of the summer but her feelings of longing for something she cannot quite describe feel like spring fever. Without the corny and dated middle section where Margy imagines then-current stars Ronald Coleman, Charles Boyer, and Bing Crosby talking to her, it is a durable standard and has been recorded hundreds of times by performers including Ella Fitzgerald, Mel Tormé, and Nina Simone. But the rest of the score has not held up as well as the songs from their Broadway shows.

The moment: In an early scene, as the family is getting ready for the fair, several characters sneak into the kitchen to add more bourbon to the mincemeat, none knowing that the others have been there. But we are in on the secret, so when it is time for the judging, we are prepared for some reaction from the judge.

And fortunately, we are given the great Donald Meek. The aptly-named actor seemed born to play timid souls. He was born in Scotland and came to America with an acrobatic troupe as a teenager. He appeared in over 100 films and is best remembered for films like "You Can't Take it With You" and "Stagecoach."

The job of a character actor is in some ways tougher than the job of the star. They have only a few moments to establish a character and deliver whatever it is that character has to contribute. They have to do that in a way that is immediately convincing and hold their own with a star without detracting from the star quality. And often, as here, their performances outshine the rest of the film.

Meek approaches the mincemeat with the other judges, very serious and dignified. But the expression on his face as he samples the bourbon-soaked mincemeat is a quiet gem. He struggles to maintain his sober and impartial demeanor, but he is surprised and delighted by the alcohol-soaked flavor and emotionally -- and perhaps literally -- intoxicated by it. It is enormous fun to see the quiet little man struggle with his excitement and knowing what it will mean for Mrs. Frake and that she will never really know what made her mincemeat so successful is the extra shot of bourbon.

More from Rodgers and Hammerstein:

"The King and I"

"South Pacific"

"Flower Drum Song"

"Carousel"

"The Sound of Music"

§ § §

88

The Story of Us (1999)

A Marriage in Two Minutes

The movie: This is not a great movie, but it is better than its reputation. It was mis-marketed as a romantic comedy when it is that rarest of genres, a bittersweet exploration of the challenges of being married.

Marriage is one of the great human adventures and yet it is easier to find a movie about inter-galactic sea monsters, cavemen riding dinosaurs, or a couple of guys knocking over a bank with duct tape and a water pistol than it is to find a movie that has any idea of how to depict what goes on in a marriage. One reason is that it is much more difficult to convey the deep richness of a lifetime of shared experience than it is to show the giddy magic of that "You love me? Really! I love you! Wow!!" moment. And marriages cover a long time period, with not much drama happening for long stretches, and that is very hard to condense into two hours. It is better suited to television, where we can see relationships withstand the challenges of daily domesticity.

We get a glimpse of a truly great real-life marriage in "Julie & Julia." But it is hard to find a movie about marriage. The best example is the brilliant British film "Two for the Road," starring Audrey Hepburn and Albert Finney, which intercuts scenes of one British couple's many visits to the South of France from their first meeting through their honeymoon, early marriage, early parenting days, and painful separations (and parodied by "The Simpsons").

"The Story of Us" is a sincere, if flawed attempt to explore the way that the very things that attract people to each other can drive them apart. It is the story of Katie and Ben Jordan (Michelle Pfeiffer and Bruce Willis, both outstanding), who have been married for 15 years. When their children go to summer camp, they no longer need to pretend to be happy and they separate to figure out whether they can repair their relationship.

The moment: Movie montages are pretty standard as a way of telescoping time and showing us, usually to the tune of a pop song, time passing as couples fall in love while they frolic on the beach and buy things at farmer's markets or train for big sporting events or compete in a series of events leading up to the big one. But there is a really marvelous montage in this film that really does evoke the chaotic, kaleidoscopic bundle of highs and lows and the brutal endurance test of family life, from "it's a boy" to "the goldfish died," from "whose turn is it to drive the carpool" to "my father died." Director Rob Reiner and his screenwriters and producers pooled their own stories to create the screenplay here, which explains why it is so messy. But it also explains why moments like the montage feel so real.

More Michelle Pfeiffer:

"Married to the Mob"

"Hairspray"

"I Could Never Be Your Woman"

"Frankie and Johnny"

§ § §

89

Stranger Than Fiction (2006)

An Existential Dilemma

The movie: With "Stranger than Fiction," first-time screenwriter Zach Hahn broke the fourth wall with a meta-narrative about a mild-mannered IRS auditor named Harold Crick (Will Ferrell) who discovers he is a character in a story. He hears a voice in his head, but it is not the kind that is an indicator of psychosis. As he says, "the voice isn't telling me to do anything. It's telling me what I've already done... accurately, and with a better vocabulary." Like the audience, Harold Crick can hear the voice-over narrating his story, the crisp English voice of Emma Thompson. And that is what makes an otherwise dull man very interesting. Many of us have had some sort of emotional or spiritual alarm clock wake us up out of our daily life and make us realize we want to make a change. Harold Crick's is just more literal than most.

This is an underrated gem of a movie, brimming with wit, charm, and insight, and with wonderful performances from Ferrell and Maggie Gyllenhaal as Ana Pascal, the Harvard Law student-turned baker he is auditing. It is filled with sweet and wonderful moments like Crick's singing Wreckless Eric's "Whole Wide World" to Pascal (yes, the choice of her name is meaningful) after her brings her flours (not flowers). And it engages surprisingly bracingly and substantively with dilemmas about balancing work, life, art, meaning, and love. And death and taxes.

The moment: One of the film's meta points has to do with the role of one of the most frequent characters in stories: the wise counselor whose assistance is sought by the hero (see "The April Fools"). Seeking out these advisors is often an important element of heroic journey stories, like Obi-Wan Kenobi and Yoda in "Star Wars." After Crick has made no progress with the usual avenues he decides to seek help from a different kind of expert, a professor of literature. Dr. Jules Hilbert is played by Dustin Hoffman, who is brilliant as a scholar who cannot help but be caught up in the chance to parse a real-life story. Here he tries to figure out what story Crick might have wandered into and whether it is a comedy or a tragedy.

> *Dr. Jules Hilbert: I've devised a test. How exciting is that? Composed of 23 questions which I think might help uncover more truths about this narrator. Now Howard... Harold, these may seem silly but your candor is paramount.*
>
> *Harold Crick: Harold. Ok.*
>
> *Dr. Jules Hilbert: So. We know it's a woman's voice. The story involves your death. It's modern. It's in English and I'm assuming the author has a cursory knowledge of the city.*
>
> *Harold Crick: Sure.*
>
> *Dr. Jules Hilbert: O.k. good. Question one. Has anyone recently left any gifts outside your home? Anything. Gum, money, a large wooden horse.*
>
> *Harold Crick: I'm sorry?*
>
> *Dr. Jules Hilbert: Just answer the question.*

Harold Crick: No.

Dr. Jules Hilbert: Do you find yourself inclined to solve murder mysteries in large luxurious homes to which you, let me finish, to which you may or may not have been invited?

Harold Crick: No. No, no, no.

Dr. Jules Hilbert: Alright. On a scale of one to ten, what would you consider the likelihood you might be assassinated?

Harold Crick: Assassinated?

Dr. Jules Hilbert: One being very unlikely, ten being expecting it around every corner.

Harold Crick: I have no idea.

Dr. Jules Hilbert: O.k. let me rephrase.

[takes a deep breath]

Dr. Jules Hilbert: Are you the king of anything?

Harold Crick: Like what?

Dr. Jules Hilbert: Anything. King of the lanes at the local bowling alley.

Harold Crick: King of the lanes?

Dr. Jules Hilbert: King of the lanes, king of the trolls,

Harold Crick: King of the Trolls?

Dr. Jules Hilbert: Yes, a clandestine land found underneath your floor boards.

Harold Crick: No.

Dr. Jules Hilbert: Huh?

Harold Crick: No. That's ridiculous.

Dr. Jules Hilbert: Agreed. Let's start with ridiculous and move backwards. Now, was any part of you at one time part of something else?

Harold Crick: Like do I have someone else's arms?

Dr. Jules Hilbert: Well is it possible at one time that you were made of stone, wood, lye, varied corpse parts? Or, earth made holy by rabbinical elders?

Harold Crick: No. Look, look. I'm sorry, but what do these questions have to do with anything?

Dr. Jules Hilbert: Nothing. The only way to find out what story you're in is to determine what stories you're not in. Odd as it may seem, I've just ruled out half of Greek literature, seven fairy tales, ten Chinese fables, and determined conclusively that you are not King Hamlet, Scout Finch, Miss Marple, Frankenstein's Monster, or a golem. Hmm? Aren't you relieved to know you're not a golem?

Harold Crick: Yes. I am relieved to know that I am not a golem.

Dr. Jules Hilbert: Good. Do you have magical powers?

The exchange is a brilliant analysis of narrative and literature. And the idea of starting with the ridiculous and moving backwards is actually quite sound.

More literary analysis of real-life situations:

"I Heart Huckabee's" (with Hoffman as an "existential detective")

"17 Again" (Thomas Lennon considers the various myths and curses that might have caused his friend to revert to his 17-year-old self)

§ § §

90

Strangers on a Train (1951)

The Tennis Game

The movie: Alfred Hitchcock studied art in school and began his career making title cards for silent films. This background is part of what made him a master of visual storytelling. His films have some vivid characters and clever dialogue, but what everyone remembers are his powerful images. The glowing glass of milk Cary Grant carries up the stairs in "Suspicion" literally had a light bulb inside of it. "Psycho" was shot in black and white but the shower scene had a few frames in red, not enough to register consciously but enough to deepen the viewer's impression of the goriness of the scene - despite never showing the knife piercing the skin.

"Strangers on a Train," based on the novel by Patricia Highsmith and with a script co-written by Raymond Chandler, is the story of a tennis champion (Farley Granger as Guy) who meets a fan (Robert Walker as Bruno) on a train ride. Bruno is more than a fan. Today we might call him a stalker. Bruno seems to know all about Guy, including a messy situation with Guy's wife, who is unfaithful but refuses to give him a divorce. Bruno tells Guy about his own problems with his father and proposes that they swap murders. If Bruno kills Guy's wife and Guy kills Bruno's father, there will be no ties between the perpetrator and the victim and so no one will suspect them.

Guy is suitably horrified. He tries to extricate himself

without an explicit refusal, perhaps because he is courteous, perhaps because he does not want to agitate a clearly disturbed man. Bruno kills Guy's wife. And he threatens to implicate Guy in the murder if he does not kill Bruno's father.

Hitchcock uses shots of crisscrossing train tracks and shows us feet walking one way and then the other to establish a sense of urgency and intersection. We see Bruno's and Guy's feet collide before we see who they are.

Themes of duality are subtly reinforced visually throughout the film, aided by the casting. Granger and Walker both conveyed a vulnerable instability and they shared the same kind of prettiness that often had them cast as characters who were weak. In addition to his usual appearance in a cameo on screen (we see him boarding the train carrying a double bass), Hitchcock's own daughter appears in the film as the outspoken younger sister of the Senator's daughter Guy wants to marry. She is similar in appearance to Guy's wife, with almost-identical glasses, triggering an emotional reaction in the unstable Bruno.

The moment: There are several suspenseful scenes in the movie, but the most powerful is the tennis match. Guy is competing in a professional game in a huge stadium filled with fans. Bruno is blackmailing Guy by threatening to leave Guy's lighter at the crime scene. So Guy is desperate to finish the game and get out so he can retrieve the lighter first. Hitchcock plays with the time a little here, speeding it up (as he slows it slightly later, when Guy is in Bruno's house). We feel the pressure on Guy, which seems to be the point of the scene. But it is about to get creepier.

Back up in the stands, the attendees are utterly absorbed in the game. Their heads swing back and forth in unison, following the ball. Except for one. In a goosebump-inducing shot, in the midst of hundreds of heads turning back and forth to watch the game, we see that Bruno sits there, completely still, intently focused on just one person, Guy.

Walker made this film just after spending time in a psychiatric hospital. Whether this gave him a chance for observation of other patients or an understanding of his own instability, his portrayal of a highly-strung sociopath is by far his best performance, even when all he has to do is sit there.

More exciting train movies:

"North by Northwest"

"Unstoppable"

"The Lady Vanishes"

"Narrow Margin"

"Murder on the Orient Express"

§ § §

91

STUCK ON YOU
(2003)

Meryl Streep Gets Silly

The movie: Meryl Streep (born Mary Louise - Meryl is a family nickname) is by any measure the most acclaimed actress of the past 30 years. She has had a record-breaking 16 Oscar nominations and three wins, for the depressed mother who leaves her family in "Kramer vs. Kramer," the concentration camp survivor in "Sophie's Choice," and Margaret Thatcher in "The Iron Lady." She holds the record for Golden Globe nominations with 27, including eight wins. Her ability to master any language or accent is legendary: Danish in "Out of Africa," Midwestern US in "Prairie Home Companion," Julia Child's upper class California trill in "Julie & Julia," Polish in "Sophie's Choice," and Australian in "A Cry in the Dark." Even when she faultlessly portrays a real life character whose mannerisms and tone are well known, like Childs and Thatcher, it is never an impression or a caricature. She has an unparalleled ability to inhabit a character fully without hiding so deep within that we cannot see what she is thinking. She is one of the very few women in Hollywood who has not had plastic surgery and her face is increasingly lovely and expressive and real.

Streep can do Shakespeare and period drama. She can play real-life characters. She played a fictional nun in "Doubt" and a fictionalized magazine editor in "The Devil Wears Prada." Both were exceptionally tough women who could be harsh but each was utterly distinct and vivid and unique. She has appeared opposite Jack Nicholson twice, as a neurotic New York food writer in "Heartburn" and as a homeless, terminally ill woman in "Ironweed," and opposite Robert De Niro three times in "The Deer Hunter," the underrated "Falling in Love," and "Marvin's Room." In each she created not just a different character but a completely different relationship dynamic with her co-star. She was an Italian war bride in a version of "The Bridges of Madison County" that vastly outdid the novel in large part due to her luminous performance. She provided the voice for an animated vixen married to George Clooney's "Fantastic Mr. Fox." She can even sing. Each of these performances was stirring, enthralling, impeccable.

But I have to say what I love most is when she does comedy. She was adorable in "It's Complicated" as a woman pulled back into an affair with her ex. But she is irresistible when she takes on really wild, over the top, crazy comedy, at the level of Lucy with the candy conveyor belt or Carol Burnett in Scarlett O'Hara's curtain dress. In "Death Becomes Her," Streep plays Madeline, a vain and selfish actress who stole her best friend Helen's beau. (Yes, they call each other Mad and Hel.) Her confrontations with Goldie Hawn as Hel are magnificently funny but the best moments are when Madeline first tries the serum that will restore her youth. Her deadpan, businesslike response to the financial portion of the deal is followed by her exquisite delight in finding herself once again looking like she is in her 20's. In the otherwise forgettable American version of "She-Devil," opposite Rosanne, Streep plays a deliciously pampered best-selling author who becomes the target of a revenge plot. And in an outrageously raunchy comedy from the Farrelly brothers ("There's Something About Mary"), Streep plays, well, herself, sort of.

"Stuck on You" is the story of co-joined twins named Bob and Walt played by Matt Damon and Greg Kinnear. Bob is very shy. Walt is an extrovert who wants to be an actor, but cannot go on stage without dragging his reluctant brother along. And no one wants to cast him anyway. Streep and her "Silkwood" co-star Cher (also terrific) play themselves and they encounter the brothers as Walt tries to break into show business.

It is a silly comedy with great performances, a lot of heart and some shrewd and incisive moments. And it is very good to see the Farrelly's commitment to including disabled characters and performers. There is a deeply moving speech of appreciation over the end credits from one of the actors.

The moment: At the very end of the film, Streep shows up to co-star with Walt in a musical version of "Bonnie and Clyde." We see a brief scene that has Streep playing herself playing the outlaw Bonnie Parker playing a musical performer, and the real Streep throws herself into it with brio and good humor. It is both touching and hilarious, and surprisingly tuneful!

More Meryl:

"Postcards from the Edge"

"Mamma Mia"

§ § §

92

The Tall Guy
(1989)

Underpants Sing a Song of Love

The movie: "The Tall Guy" would be worth watching just because it is the feature film debut of screenwriter Richard Curtis ("Four Weddings and a Funeral") and actress Emma Thompson ("Sense and Sensibility," "Howards End," "The Remains of the Day"). It was also the first film for Jason Isaacs (Lucius Malfoy in the "Harry Potter" films) and director Mel Smith. Although it is uneven, it is also a lot of fun and more than two decades later the wildly goofy comedy makes up for the portions that do not work very well.

Jeff Goldblum plays Dexter, an American actor living in England. He works as the foil to an imperious and self-important comic named Ron Anderson (Rowan Atkinson). Dexter's primary contribution is to be a visual joke. He lives in a little apartment and his landlady is a benign but distracted presence with a parade of lovers, sometimes several at once.

Dexter meets a pretty nurse named Kate Lemon (Thompson) in the emergency room. He makes up a trip to Morocco so that he can keep coming back for shots. Finally he asks her out. Things go very well until they don't, when Dexter is cast in a preposterous new musical version of "The Elephant Man" (a very funny poke at Andrew Lloyd Webber) and has a dalliance with a co-star.

The moment: Often when a movie couple first fall in love there is a musical montage showing the couple cooking together and laughing in the rain to a forgettable pop song. Smith and Curtis create a lulu here with a very distinctive montage that both tweaks and transcends the usual clichés. The usual montage is not self-aware. The people in it do not know that they are in a movie montage.

They know in this one. When Dexter and Lemon get together, there is an utterly charming series of clips that includes everyone cheering them on, to Labi Siffre's "It Must Be Love" performed by Madness. We get glimpses of the relationship between Kate and Dexter. She throws out his awful clothes (though they both climb into his Superman pajamas first) and they have dresser-shaking sex. The landlady and the other people in her bed (are there five?) happily sing along, as does the blind beggar outside Dexter's apartment, the entire audience at the theater Dexter works at, various other people, and surprisingly adorably, Dexter's underpants. It is funny, sweet, and a little nutty, just like falling in love.

More Richard Curtis:

"Four Weddings and a Funeral"

"Notting Hill"

"Love Actually"

"Bridget Jones' Diary"

"Pirate Radio"

§ § §

93

THIS IS SPINAL TAP (1984)

Jeanine

The movie: The American Film Institute places the fake documentary about a heavy metal band "This is Spinal Tap" as the 29th funniest American film of all time. I'd put it as number 2 (after "Some Like it Hot"). This was the first of the Christopher Guest repertory group's improvised comedies about slightly dim people who are not nearly as talented as they think they are or as important as they would like to be. It is a cultural icon with fans who happily recite it line by line.

The term "mockumentary" was created to describe Guest's films, improvised by the cast. It is not just a satire of metal music but of documentaries as well, the pastiches of archival clips and the pretense that the presence of the cameras is not affecting what they are filming.

The scene in which Guest as Nigel Tufnel explains that he had special amps made that "go to eleven" is one of the funniest ever filmed and the movie is filled with moments of pure comic genius, from the miscommunication about the size of the Stonehenge replica ("There's such a fine line between clever and stupid"), to the mysterious deaths of all of their drummers, the awful "Smell the Glove" cover art that gets rejected by the label, the fruitless journey through the labyrinths under the Cleveland performance space to try to find the stage, like something between Kafka and Beckett, the cameos from Billy Crystal, Fran Drescher, Fred Willard, Howard Hesseman and more, and the appearance by director Rob Reiner as the documentary director Marty DiBergi, nodding sagely as though he has a transcendently insightful appreciation for the group's oeuvre.

And the oeuvre itself is note-perfect. It is hard to be more over-the-top than real-life metal bands, but Spinal Tap delivers with songs like "Big Bottom"("talk about mudflaps, my girl's got 'em") and "Tonight I'm Gonna Rock You Tonight" are headbanger-worthy and hilarious. Guest and his collaborators Harry Shearer and Michael McKean are equally deft in other musical genres as well. In this film we get a chance to hear snippets of the group's pre-metal releases as skiffle and pop/hippie bands, in "Waiting for Guffman" they did show tunes, and in "A Mighty Wind" they wrote folk songs that sounded authentic and genuinely touching. The affection Guest and his repertory group have for their characters' aspirations to express themselves and to be appreciated gives a depth to their comedy that makes the films worth watching over and over.

The moment: One moment in this film that does not get the attention it deserves is the scene where the group is complaining to their long-suffering manager, Ian Faith, played by National Lampoon editor Tony Hendra. We have already seen the different reactions the trio had to the arrival of Jeanine (June Chadwick).

Her boyfriend, David St. Hubbins (McKean) so overjoyed to see her that he does not notice the expressions of his bandmates, who clearly are not at all happy to have here there. Later, when she mistakenly refers to the Dolby audio technology as "dobbly" they are quick to use that as a way to dismiss her comments that the mix on the new album makes it impossible to hear the vocals. We get a sense of why they do not want to listen to her a moment later when she proposes a new look for the group, based on the signs of the zodiac.

A few moments later, the group seems briefly united

again in complaining to Ian and agreeing that he needs some help until David says, "Maybe there's someone already in the organization. We don't have to pay insurance. We don't have to pay extra room, etc. Since she's already here, she's already among us, and uh, she can...she is certainly capable of taking over...." The dawning realization that agreeing to get help for Ian has doomed them to more interference from Jeanine is includes great depth of understanding of what would come to be known as the "VH1 Behind the Music" syndrome of band collapse, the stresses of the road, the rivalries, and of course the girlfriends. The anguish is real but also funny and funny because it is so real.

More from the Spinal Tap crew:

"Best in Show"

"Waiting for Guffman"

"A Mighty Wind"

§ § §

94

THE THOMAS CROWN AFFAIR (1968)

The Chess Game

The movie: The original "Thomas Crown Affair" was an ultra-stylish heist movie that was less about getting the money than about getting away with it.

The first few moments of the film are a meticulously executed five-man bank robbery. We then meet Mr. Crown (Steve McQueen, moving sleekly as a jaguar, as always). He is an enormously successful business man, closing a multi-million dollar real estate deal. He smiles mirthlessly as he tells the buyer, "You overpaid."

What could be the connection? Could a man who seems to have everything risk it all to rob a bank? Vicki Anderson (Faye Dunaway) thinks so.

She is a beautiful investigator for the insurance company who arrives to conduct her own inquiries for a percentage of whatever is recovered. She guesses that Crown, who plays polo and flies a glider is the kind of thrill-seeker who would orchestrate a bank robbery just for the fun of it. "What a funny, dirty, little mind," he says to her in response to her theories. "It's a funny, dirty, little job," she tells him.

He's enough of a thrill-seeker to enjoy the risk of getting close to Vicki.

The moment: After an evening out they come back to his elegant brownstone. He sees her looking at the chessboard and asks, "Do you play?" She responds: "Try me."

Director Norman Jewison ("Moonstruck," "In the Heat of the Night") and editor Hal Ashby (who would go on to direct "Shampoo" and "Being There") then give us what is unquestionably the steamiest chess game in history, on or off screen. It is a masterpiece of editing as well as a metaphor that illuminates the larger game the two are playing. As a fire flickers in the fireplace, Dunaway's perfectly manicured fingernail touches her perfectly sculpted lower lip. Her fingers caress a chess piece, then her own skin, just barely. In eighteen moves, she is about to win when he stands, a little breathless, and says, "Let's play something else." And then, there is a swoon-worthy one-minute kissing sequence, which took a very un-romantic eight hours to film over a period of several days.

More chess scenes in movies:

"The Luzhin Defense" John Turturro stars in a film based on a novella by Vladimir Nabokov about a chess champion struggling to maintain his sanity.

"Searching for Bobby Fischer" An eight-year-old becomes a chess champion in this story of a family's effort to support their son's gift without distorting his perspective in this brilliantly acted film based on the true story of the son of sportswriter Fred Waitzkin.

"The Seventh Seal" This Ingmar Bergman film includes an iconic (and much-parodied) scene with a knight playing a chess game with Death.

§ § §

95

A Thousand Clowns
(1965)

Apology

The movie: "A Thousand Clowns" is one unforgettable movie moment after another, starting with a galvanizing opening scene. Jason Robards, Gene Saks, Barry Gordon, and William Daniels repeat their Broadway roles in this adaptation of Herb Gardner's 1962 play about an iconoclastic New Yorker who is caring for his 12-year-old nephew. One thing I love about this movie is the way it has served as a measure of where I am. I have watched it every few years since it came out when I was in middle school and every time I have a different reaction to the decision the main character makes at the end.

Ralph Rosenblum's wonderful book about his career as an editor, *When the Shooting Stops…the Cutting Begins*, has a chapter on making this film. He describes his experience working with Gardner who came in after the film had been cut very conventionally and insisted he start over, because it was too much like a play and appeared static and theatrical. Rosenblum was used to working with directors who were precise and efficient. Gardner would watch the same footage all day. He recorded Robards singing and playing for hours, sent the cinematographer out to get new footage of people going to work and replaced dialogue with a bicycle-riding montage. Dozens, maybe hundreds of movies copied that technique. The improvisational, jazz-inspired rhythms of the cutting brought the movie to life.

I love the scene where Murray Burns (Robards) explains to visiting social workers about how his nephew (Gordon) came to live with him. The boy's mother, he says, has a philosophy of life "somewhere to the left of 'Whoopee!'" and "communicates with us almost entirely by rumor." He explains why the boy they call Nick does not really have a legal name.

> *I made a deal with him when he was six, up to which time he was known rather casually as "Chubby," that he could try out any name he wished, for as long as he wished, until his thirteenth birthday, at which point he would have to decide on a name he liked permanently. He went through a long period of dogs' names when he was still little, "Rover" and "King" having a real vogue there for a while. For three months, he referred to himself as "Big Sam," then there was Little Max, Snoopy, Chip, Rock, Rex, Mike, Marty, Lamont, Chevrolet, Wyatt, Fred, Phil, Woodrow, Lefty, the Phantom. He received his library card last year in the name Raphael Sabatini, his Cub Scout membership lists him as Dr. Morris Fishbein, and only last week a friend called asking if Toulouse could come over to his house for dinner. "Nick" seems to be the one that will stick, though.*

The movie wisely grants dignity to the characters that Burns dismisses too easily as fatally unimaginative and captured by convention. Daniels' social worker character has a very touching speech about how he envies Burns for being one of "the warm people." And Martin Balsam won an Oscar as Burns' more responsible brother, who explains that he does not want to shake up the world. He has, he says, "a talent for surrender" but takes pride in being "the best possible Arnold Burns." He has just one request. "Allow me once to leave a room before you do." Gardner and director Fred Coe show us that the moral superiority of snark has costs and responsibility has a purpose.

Then there's the exquisite performance of Barbara Harris as Sandra, the vulnerable young social work trainee. Her awkward befuddlement the morning after she spends the night with Burns, making polite conversation about coffee, is beautifully done.

The moment: Later, Burns has failed to do something he promised. He tells Sandra he stood on a street corner practicing his apology. What surprised him was how many passers-by felt wronged enough to assume he was apologizing to them and were gracious enough to accept it.

> It was fabulous. I had tapped some vast reservoir. Something had happened to all of them for which they felt somebody should apologize. If you went up to people on the street and offered them money, they'd refuse it. But everybody accepts apology immediately. It is the most negotiable currency. I said to them "I am sorry" and they were all so generous, so kind. You could give 'em love and it wouldn't be accepted half as graciously, as unquestioningly. I could run up on the roof right now and holler "I am sorry" and half a million people would holler right back, "That's O.K. just see that you don't do it again!" That's the most you should expect from life, a really good apology.

More classic movie apologies:

John Cleese in "A Fish Called Wanda"

Steve McQueen in "Love With a Proper Stranger"

Tom Cruise in "Jerry Maguire"

§ § §

96

Top Gun
(1986)

DBTA

The movie: DBTA stands for "dead by third act." That describes the character who might as well be wearing a sign: "My job in this movie is to die so the hero or heroine can have a learning experience." This is not new to movies. Books like *Little Women, The Grapes of Wrath,* and *To Kill a Mockingbird* (all with memorable movie adaptations) use the loss of important characters as a crucial element in the lead's progress to adulthood and mature understanding. Think of what "Four Weddings and a Funeral" would be without the funeral or the impact of the losses of beloved animals in "Old Yeller" and "The Yearling." In some cases, the DBTA is a flawed character whose death is redemptive or inspiring, like Ronald Reagan's "Gipper" in "Knute Rockne, All American."

In other stories there is a loss that is a symbolic death. In *Pride and Prejudice*, Elizabeth Bennett's sister loses her reputation by running off with a soldier without getting married. In "The King's Speech," it is the end of Bertie's comparatively quiet life when his brother abdicates the throne. Sometimes, heroes witness the death of an idealized vision of their community or the way the world works as a turning point. Think of "Erin Brockovich" or "Schindler's List."

A classic DBTA has to demonstrate his or her importance to the lead very quickly and be so appealing that we, too, feel the loss. In "Fried Green Tomatoes," Chris O'Donnell plays Buddy, the older brother of Idgie (Mary Stuart Masterson), the tomboyish youngest child of a Southern family in the 1920's. Buddy is the only one who understands her and loves her for who she is. In the first ten minutes of the film he creates a character so completely wonderful that if he does not get out of the way fast, there will be no story because there will be no struggle for her to overcome. He is a rare DBFA ("dead by first act"), killed within the first few moments of the film, and it is a tribute to his performance that he is able to make such a strong impression in a brief scene.

"Top Gun" is the story of a superb but cocky and impulsive fighter pilot with the call sign Maverick (Tom Cruise) who has some growing up to do. And there's no better way to inspire a character to grow up than to see how serious life and death can be.

The moment: Enter one of the great DBTAs in the history of film: Maverick's friend Goose in "Top Gun." Anthony Edwards plays Nick Bradshaw, the Radar Intercept Officer who flies with Naval Aviator pilot Pete Mitchell. Their call signs, "Goose" and "Maverick," are indicators of their natures. Goose is affable, easygoing, and tolerant of Maverick's impetuous antics, perhaps even envious of his willingness to break the rules. It is clear he is a goner, though, when we see him with his adorable wife (pre-stardom Meg Ryan) and child, banging away at a piano and singing (badly) "Great Balls of Fire." He is just too perfect. There is nowhere for him to go in the story except to be sacrificed so that Maverick can be forced to confront the consequences of being a hot-head (even though he is formally found not to have caused the accident) and Goose's death will allow Maverick to emerge, sadder, wiser, more responsible, and more determined.

Other classic DBTAs:

    Charley in "On the Waterfront"

    Riff and Bernardo in "West Side Story"

    Plato in "Rebel Without a Cause"

    The title character in "Mr. Roberts"

§ § §

97

Toy Story 3
(2010)

The Sky

The movie: Sequels are almost always a disappointment. The few that work were invariably part of an organic original concept, like "Godfather II," "The Empire Strikes Back," and the Harry Potter films. When a story is intended to be over at the end of the movie and then the suits start running the numbers and order up a sequel before there is a script, it is off to a bad start. Five reasons that sequels rarely work:

1. The characters and storyline can never be new again. A large part of the appeal of the original was its freshness and that advantage is gone.

2. Successful people do not always know what made them successful the first time.

3. When people have been enormously successful, no one wants to say "no" to them. So they get cut off from feedback that could make the film better.

4. People stay the same when the world changes around them. What worked at one time may not work even six months later.

5. The people responsible for enormously successful works of art are exceptionally imaginative. They do not want to repeat themselves. So they often move on to exciting new projects and the people who are satisfied trying to replicate someone else's idea take over.

And there are even more reasons that a second sequel to Pixar's first feature film should not have worked. The original came out in 1995. A sequel intended for lesser straight-to-video release four years later turned out to be unexpectedly high quality and ended up being shown in theaters. There was no plan to create a third chapter for astronaut Buzz Lightyear and cowboy Woody. And when Pixar decided to make a third movie nearly a decade later, they turned it over to Michael Arndt, whose only other screenplay was "Little Miss Sunshine." He became the first screenwriter to be nominated for Oscars for both of his first two films.

It turned out to be a one-in-a-million third chapter that was even better than its superb predecessors. As the Pixar crew grew older and more thoughtful, the themes of their movies became deeper and more ambitious. The first five minutes of "Toy Story 3" contain one of the most joyous tributes to the power of imagination ever created. And then we see a story as wise about love and family and the meaning of life as any live action film ever made.

We first met Andy as a child in the original "Toy Story." Seeing him prepare for college and literally put away childish things is almost unbearably poignant. So is seeing the toys try to create meaning for themselves, knowing that their reason for being must end. When, thinking they are about to be incinerated, they reach for each other's hands, it is as moving and as real to us as any live action film.

The moment: I am indebted to Deacon Greg Kandra of Beliefnet for pointing out that "the last shot of 'Toy Story 3' is the first shot of the original film: a blue sky dotted by clouds. But in the first film, it's a sky painted on Andy's bedroom wall. Here, at the conclusion of the third film, it's the real sky of the real world - or, at least, Pixar's real world - suggesting limitless adventures out there that are awaiting the little boy who grew up, and moved on." Perfect.

More Pixar classics:

"Toy Story"

"Toy Story 2"

"A Bug's Life"

"Monsters, Inc."

"Finding Nemo"

§ § §

98

Twelve Monkeys
(1995)

Brad Pitt Gives a Tour

The movie: Terry Gilliam's dystopic sci-fi vision is based on a 1962 short film called "La Jetée" ("the pier") from French director Chris Marker.

In a future where most of the human population has been wiped out by a virus and the survivors live underground, a prisoner named James Cole (Bruce Willis) is sent back in time to see if he can find the original virus so that scientists can come up with a cure. Instead, he tries to prevent the spread of the virus by tracking down the people he thinks are behind it, an activist group called The Army of the Twelve Monkeys, and at one point he ends up in a mental hospital, where he meets another patient played by Brad Pitt.

In "Tropic Thunder," Robert Downey, Jr. hilariously lampoons the fascination actors have for playing disabled characters. While his comments are outrageous (after all, this is an over-the-top, intentionally provocative comedy and they are coming from a character who is a white Australian actor playing a black American), his criticism of the too-often show-boating, awards-baiting performances from actors playing developmentally disabled or mentally ill characters is more than fair. Most frequently, actors seem to wink at the audience as if to say, "Look at how humble I am to hide all of my talent and glamour inside this limited character." They get some of the external details right, but they hold on to their real-life screen presence just to make sure we realize that it is acting.

Brad Pitt is different. No actor has ever been better at understanding and deploying his natural star power than Pitt. Former MGM head Dore Schary used to call it "motor," that indefinable something that has nothing to do with looks or acting ability or off-screen appeal but is the quality that grabs our attention and defines what it means to be a movie star. Some people are actors, some are movie stars, and some are lucky enough to be both. Pitt is not only both; he has the rare ability to decide from movie to movie how much of each he will deploy in the mixture he uses to create his performance. He is as comfortable as a leading man as he is a character actor. He does both equally well and knows how to combine them when he wants to. In this movie, he gives one of the most fearless, specific, and authentic performances ever filmed of a bright man struggling with mental illness and there is not a hint of acting class showing-off.

Pitt told *Entertainment Weekly* that to prepare himself for the role he watched the searing documentary "Titticut Follies" and "anything with Dennis Hopper" to find what he

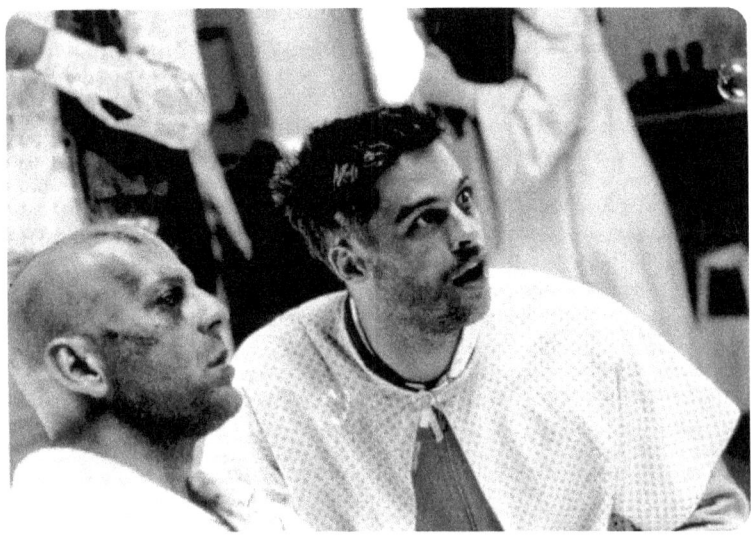

needed for the character. He was critical of his performance. "I nailed the first half of the movie and I dogged the second half. I rode the gimmick. I rode the manic. A year and a half later I woke up in the middle of the night and went, 'That's what it was.' I played it all manic, and that was a mistake."

The moment: When Cole is sent to a mental hospital, an orderly asks a patient, Jeffrey Goines (Pitt), to show him around. This is the kind of part that the "Austin Powers" films amusingly personify as "Basil Exposition," the character who is explaining to the audience as well as to the hero the information we need to understand the situation and lay the foundation for what lies ahead. These conversations can be tedious, but Pitt manages to get across the information we need, the most important being the atmosphere as well as the operations of the mental hospital, and his performance also resonates with sense of disturbance and madness at the heart of the tone and themes of the film.

When Goines asks how much he will be paid for the tour, the orderly says, "Five thousand dollars, my man. That enough? I'll wire it to your account as usual, okay?" Goines agrees as the orderly chuckles and walks away, thinking he has once again put something over on the poor deluded mental patient, and perhaps we do, too, until Goines says to Cole confidentially, "Kid around, kid around. It makes them feel good, we're all pals. We're prisoners, they're the guards, but it's all in good fun, you see?"

Each statement he makes seems to have a prismatic, splintered reality. Pitt displays a kaleidoscopic array of comments and twitches as we see the dozens of small battles inside him to maintain coherence and control, and, of course, it takes an actor of masterful control himself to convey all of that.

More from Brad Pitt:
  "Thelma and Louise"
  "Moneyball"
  "True Romance"

99

The Wild Parrots of Telegraph Hill (2005)

The Last Shot

The movie: Telegraph Hill, overlooking the North Beach section of San Francisco, is a place where all kinds of creatures from all kinds of places can feel welcome. One of them is onetime musician Mark Bittner, a man with "no visible means of support" who is himself the support for some of the neighborhood's most colorful residents, a flock of bright green wild parrots.

Bittner knows and loves each one of them. He is in one respect a sort of St. Francis of Telegraph Hill, carting huge bags of birdseed home on the bus to feed to them and taking the sick ones into his home to nurse them. But he is also their Jane Goodall, possibly the only person in history to study a group of parrots so intently over so long a period.

Bittner does not have a job, at least not one that pays him anything. He lives rent-free in a crumbling cottage and gets free pastries from a local cafe. The birds are his full-time job. He studies them, reads up on them, consults the bird specialist at the local zoo, and develops his own treatments, even grooming one parrot who no longer has a mate to do it for him.

The moment: Through Bittner, even the least animal-friendly viewer will begin to fall in love with these brave and beautiful birds. His passion, dedication, and understanding are first impressive, then touching, then transcendent as he begins to talk about the death of a beloved parrot named Tupelo and tells a story from a Zen master about the way we are all connected. The movie's conclusion is a moment of breathtaking perfection -- the sweetest connection of all. I can't say more without spoiling the surprise.

More animal documentaries:

"March of the Penguins"

"Born to be Wild"

"Winged Migration"

§ § §

100

Wives and Lovers
(1963)

Eating a Tuna Sandwich

The movie: "Wives and Lovers" is probably better remembered for inspiring a Burt Bachrach/Hal David song that does not appear anywhere in the movie than for its lightweight story about the impact of success on a writer and his family. Van Johnson plays Bill, sheepishly relying on his wife's paychecks from her job as a dental hygienist and making do with free-lance jobs like writing a cookbook while he waits to see if Lucinda, his chic and beautiful agent (Martha Hyer), can sell his novel. When Lucinda arrives with a bottle of champagne to tell Bill that she has sold his book not just to a publisher but to Broadway and the movies, Bill buys the mink coat she is wearing and presents it to his wife, Bertie (Janet Leigh) who puts her apron on over it and washes the dishes. Success goes to his head and they move out to a mansion in Connecticut while Bertie confides in the divorcée next door (Shelly Winters) and gets romanced by the star of Bill's play (Jeremy Slate). It is silly and predictable, more enjoyable as an artifact (watch Bill struggle with the high-tech of that era, his hi-fi) and for the knockout dresses from Edith Head (especially the one Bertie and Lucinda both wear to the same party) than for its story or performances.

But there is one very sweet scene that has so little to do with the rest of the movie I can only conclude it was inserted by the writer because it really happened and was too good not to include somewhere.

Two writers worked on the movie, both better known for more serious screenplays. "Wives and Lovers" is based on a play by Jay Presson Allen. She prided herself on her range and worked on a variety of film, television, and theatrical projects, though her comedies tended to be more barbed than this one. Her work included the Hitchcock film "Marnie" as well as the theatrical and movie adaptations of "The Prime of Miss Jean Brodie" and the screenplays for "Cabaret," "Travels With My Aunt," and, with director Sidney Lumet, "Prince of the City." Her play, "The First Wife," was adapted by two-time Oscar winner Edward Anhalt ("Becket" and "Panic in the Streets").

The moment: "Can I make a tuna sandwich?" Julie (Claire Wilcox) asks her dad Bill (Van Johnson), who is working on his typewriter in their cramped tenement apartment. Julie is 7¾ years old. Bill distractedly gives her his permission, and then realizes, with horrified fascination, that her idea of making a tuna fish sandwich is to put four small plates on the table, place lettuce on one, tuna on one, mayonnaise on one, and bread on one, and then take a pinch of each with her fingers and put it in her mouth.

Any parent will identify with Bill's inability to prevent himself from making the obvious comment and asking her what she is doing. She looks up at him as though he is a little slow and explains she is eating a tuna fish sandwich. Again, knowing he probably should not, he explains that most people combine the ingredients, and she tells him she does not like to have her foods touch each other. Like every parent going back to the cave days, when Cro-Magnon patiently explained that wooly mammoth tastes better when it is combined with some greens, Bill tells Julie that when it all gets to her stomach, it will be touching, and she says with a little shudder, "I don't want to hear it."

Later in the film, Bill takes Julie to Sardi's. She does the same thing with a peanut butter and jelly sandwich and it is just as charming.

More father-daughter scenes:

"Papa's Delicate Condition"

"A Little Princess"

"Fly Away Home"

"To Kill a Mockingbird"

101

WORKING GIRL
(1988)

The Best BFF

The movie: I once interviewed a Disney animator who told me that he resolved that if he was put in charge of a movie, the lead human character would not have a cute animal sidekick. It had just been done so many times. But then when he did get a chance, he realized why the hero or heroine has to have a cute animal sidekick. Otherwise, they would have to talk to themselves.

The Little Mermaid talks to a flounder and a crab. Cinderella has the mice Gus Gus and Jacques, not only good confidantes but with lady friends who are very handy with a needle and thread. Aladdin has a monkey and his nemesis, Jafar, has a parrot. In "Tangled," Rapunzel has a chameleon. These relationships not only give us a chance to find out what the lead characters are thinking. They give us a chance to see their kindness and good spirits. Fish, reptiles, mice, and birds are not going to sing songs and create haute couture for just anyone.

The equivalent in live-action movies is the wisecracking best friend. In the old days, the best friend role usually went to Eve Arden. She often played the worldly, cynical, heart-of-gold, forever loyal type who had few illusions but had not lost hope. Some of her best roles were in "Anatomy of a Murder," "Mildred Pierce," "Stage Door," "My Reputation," and "One for the Book."

The best friend is usually attractive but not beautiful.

Sometimes he or she will merit a B-story arc or romance to support or contrast with whatever the lead character is going through, but mostly the job is to listen sympathetically, make a quip to break the tension and cheer everyone up, and generally to provide support and some comic relief. In recent years, the terrific actress Judy Greer has played best friend to too many Jennifers and Jessicas and been the best thing in too many second-rate romantic comedies.

There are male best friends as well, of course, from Tonto in "The Lone Ranger" to Van Johnson in "Brigadoon" and "Yours, Mine, and Ours," to everyone but Vince in "Entourage."

My favorite modern movie best friend has to be Joan Cusack. Starting as a teenager in "My Bodyguard," she has exemplified the best of the long tradition of movie best friends to Julia Roberts ("The Runaway Bride"), Kate Hudson ("Raising Helen," where she was technically a sister) and even "Say Anything" (where played the sister of her real-life brother John Cusack). Joan Cusack has also played a villain in "Adams Family Values," and the love interest in "School of Rock" and the underrated "My Blue Heaven." But her best role was as Melanie Griffith's best friend in "Working Girl."

It is a Cinderella story of a secretary who dreams of doing deals on Wall Street, starring Melanie Griffith in her best performance. It is deftly directed by Mike Nichols, whose many assets include his being so all-around wonderful that everyone wants to work with him. Every role down to the one-line parts is impeccably cast; after all, this is a movie where the only person to appear in six of the then top-10 box office champions of all times plays a supporting role: Harrison Ford as the love interest.

And Joan Cusack plays the engaged best friend of the lead character, who provides sympathy, support, and a reality check, all while sporting big, big hair and a Crayola box of colors on her eyelids and tawking like she neva left Staten

Island. And when she gets her friend's good news at the end of the film, her joy in the final shot is the perfect ending.

The moment: Tess McGill (Griffith) is pretending to be her own boss and Jack Trainer (Ford), the man she hopes to work with on her project, has just shown up at the office. She can't let him see her sitting at a secretary's desk, so she implores her best friend Cyn (Cusack) to "be me," to pretend to be McGill's secretary and show him into what they will pretend is her office. Cusack is a treat to watch as she escorts Trainer. While she is exaggeratedly obsequious and overly familiar, she is hilariously incapable of any pretense and enjoying herself enormously. She was nominated for an Oscar and won a Golden Globe for her performance.

More warm but wisecracking best friends:

Helen Broderick in "Top Hat" and "Swing Time"

Rupert Everett in "My Best Friend's Wedding"

Carrie Fisher in "When Harry Met Sally"

§ § §

Acknowledgements

I am grateful every day to those who give me a place to write about movies, especially Beliefnet, and to Sharon Hoffman, Laura Emerick, David Burke, and Matt Atchity, and to the friends who invite me on the radio each week to talk about the week's new releases. I hope I get to work with Zachary Cloyd on all my books. His kind offer of help after all the hard work he did on my last book defines what it means to go above and beyond the call of duty. Alyssa Machold Ellsworth is an expert on movies and writing and a dear friend who kindly read through the manuscript and gave me thoughtful comments. Many thanks to Daniel Castillo for his beautiful design work on the book and for always going beyond my highest expectations.

Roger Ebert has inspired me since his very first review appeared in the Chicago Sun-Times and he and Chaz Ebert have been a wonderful source of friendship and support. Roger's far-flung critics and On Demanders have become good friends, especially Odie Henderson, Omar Moore, Omer Mozaffer, Anath White, and Michał Oleszczyk.

The best part of writing a book is the opportunity to give a shout-out to my beloved friends and family. Thanks and love to my wonderful parents and sisters and all of the Minow and Apatoff families, my friends Kristie Miller, Patty Marx, Jeff Sonnenfeld, David and Marcie Drew, Toby, Bhupinder, Kabir, and Joven Kent, Tim, Caroline, and Arlo Kent, Jesse Norman and his family, Lilah Lohr, Daniel and Matthew Ornstein and their parents, Bobbi Wade, Michael O'Sullivan, the Anthes-Mayer family, Alexandra Burguieres, Adam Frankel and Stephanie Psaki, A. T. Palmer, Steve Lawrence, Andy Borowitz, Tom Dunkel, Robert Elisberg, Judy Viorst, Jim Cheng, Judy Pomeranz, Cynthea Riesenberg, Kathy and

Andrew Stephen, Mary, Richard, Jack, and Neal Kelly, Elizabeth, David, and Riley Alberding, Nadine Prosperi, Deborah Baughman, Jon Friedman, Tracy and Kathy in Wichita, Monty and the gang in Pittsburgh, Jeff, Jer, Laura, and Tommy in San Diego, Lori, Jeff, and Meredith in Portland, Ron Olson, Liza Mundy, Paul Zelinsky and Deborah Hallen, Deborah Davidson, Kayla Gillan, Shannon Hackett, Beth Young, Ann Yerger, Terry Savage, Bill Pedersen, Gary Waxman, the Mandel-Robinson family, Adam Bernstein, the Bingham-Kavenaugh family, Jane Leavy, Eleonor Peralta, Steve Wallman, Sam Natapoff, Steve Waldman and Amy Cunningham, Michael Kinsley, Parvané Hashemi, Bill O'Sullivan, Ken Suslick, Ellen, Sandy, and Elyse Twaddell, Steve Friess, Raffaela Wakeman, Duncan Clark, Ellen Burka, Michael Deal, Ivory Zorich, and Stuart Brotman.

Thanks to my movie pals Tim Gordon, Ivan Walks, Brandon Fibbs, Jack Giroux, Tricia Olszewski, John Hanlon, Jeanette Catsoulis, Dan Kois, Christopher Orr, Kevin McCarthy, Josh Hylton, Jen Chaney, William Ayres, Matthew Razek, Christian Toto, Chuck Rich, Dean Rogers, Dustin Putman, Patrick Jennings, Eli and Andrea Savada, Jay Carr, Willie Waffle, Travis Hopson, John Nolan, Rebecca Causey, Sandie Angulo Chen, Alan Zilberman, Cindy Fuchs, Jim Judy, and Nick Digilio. Extra special thanks to movie experts and great friends Desson Thomson, Mike Clark, and Mark Jenkins for their guidance, support, and feedback. Warm thoughts to the late Joe Barber, much missed.

I am also very grateful to everyone at Allied-THA, especially my friends Sara Taylor, Gloria Jones, Wendie Vestfall, Emilia Stefanczyk, Liz Malek, Monica Palenzuela, and Maggie Haslem, to Laine Kaplowitz of Landmark and Renée Tsao of PR Collaborative and my pal Dre Birscovich. Special thanks to Rosemary Hanes and the staff at the motion picture collection of the Library of Congress for making the hardest-to-find films available. Thanks, as ever, to Bob Monks, the source of inspiration and support for a quarter of a century, and to all of my partners at GMI.

Most of all, I want to thank my family - my children, Benjamin and Rachel, and my husband David, still the best person I know.

About the Author

Nell Minow reviews movies and DVD/Blu-Ray/Streaming releases each week for Beliefnet at moviemom.com and on radio stations across the country. Her features, interviews, and commentary about movies, media, popular culture, and values have appeared in the Chicago Sun-Times, the Chicago Tribune, USA Today, Parents, and many other publications. She is the author of *The Movie Mom's Guide to Family Movies* and the *Must-See Movies* series of e-books.

Miniver Press is a publisher of lively and informative non-fiction books about culture and history. Purchasers of this book may request a free ebook in the "must-see movie" series. Write to editor@ miniverpress.com for your copy.

§ § §

www.ingramcontent.com/pod-product-compliance
Lightning Source LLC
LaVergne TN
LVHW051108080426
835510LV00018B/1950